............*A Balanced Life*

A Balanced Life

9 Strategies for Coping with the Mental Health Problems of a Loved One

TOM SMITH

. . . .

HAZELDEN

Hazelden
Center City, Minnesota 55012
hazelden.org

Library of Congress Cataloging-in-Publication Data
Smith, Tom, 1940–
     A balanced life : nine strategies for coping with the mental health
problems of a loved one / Tom Smith. — 1st ed.
        p.   cm.
     ISBN-13: 978-1-59285-662-6 (softcover)
     1. Mentally ill—Care.   2. Mentally ill—Family relationships.
  3. Mentally ill—Anecdotes.   I. Title.
     RC439.5.S646 2008
     362.196'89—dc22

                                                      2008018794

Editor's note
The names, details, and circumstances may have been changed to protect
the privacy of those mentioned in this publication.
     This publication is not intended as a substitute for the advice of health
care professionals.
     Alcoholics Anonymous and AA are registered trademarks of Alcoholics
Anonymous World Services, Inc.

The content on page 34 and page 36 from *People Skills* by Robert Bolton has
been reprinted with the permission of Simon & Schuster Adult Publishing
Group. Copyright © 1979 by Simon & Schuster, Inc. All rights reserved.

12 11 10 09 08   1 2 3 4 5 6

Cover design by Theresa Gedig
Interior design by Ann Sudmeier
Typesetting by BookMobile Design and Publishing Services

To our support group, which meets on the first and third Thursday of every month:

> *You experienced and refined these strategies before they were a book. Thank you for your stories of hope, and for your inspiration, courage, and wisdom.*

..........Contents

...........Acknowledgments

This book reflects both the painful and the joyful experiences of many people who are the families and friends of a loved one with mental health problems. Through listening to their stories, many of which mirror my own life, I was encouraged to write this book. In particular, I am grateful to the members of the Karla Smith Foundation's "Hope for a Balanced Life" support group—a group for the family and friends of people with mental illness. Some of them contributed stories of hope for this book, and I appreciate their honesty in sharing their experiences and their courage in seeking solutions to difficult life situations.

Janie Bloomer, Margie Jones, and Emily Smith read an early version of this book and offered valuable input into the content, format, and style of the text. Thank you again. Fran, my wife, and Kevin, our son, lived this material with me before it became words on a page. Their love, hope, commitment, and talent gave birth to the concept, purpose, and shape of the book, and I am continually grateful to them not only for their love and support but for their very practical help in creating this book. Sid Farrar, my editor at Hazelden Publishing, provided more than an expert analysis of the text. His additions and deletions improved the material to an extent beyond my original expectations. I appreciate his expertise and also his obvious passion for the subject matter, his genuine kindness, thoughtfulness, humility, and encouragement. He is a trusted advisor, and I am blessed.

Finally, and sadly, I am grateful to my daughter, Karla. I certainly wish it were otherwise, but her struggle with bipolar disorder and her suicide introduced me, on a personal level, to the world of mental illness. This book honors her memory, as she would want it.

.........*Preface*

This book flows from my family's own experience. Our realization that this book was needed, and the eventual form it took, were shaped by our story. That story is still unfolding, but here I will share its beginnings with you.

My wife, Fran, and I had been married two years when our twins, Kevin and Karla, were born. Throughout their childhood and adolescence, we were a normal, happy, middle-class family dealing with the predictable issues of family life and parenting.

Then, very suddenly in January 1996, when Karla was nineteen and beginning the second semester of her sophomore year in college, she fell into her first major depression. She abandoned school, came home, crawled beneath the covers of her bed, and barely left her room.

We sought help from a psychiatrist and a counselor. With medication and counseling, Karla eventually came out of the depression, but only after her first suicide attempt. In the summer and fall of 1998, she experienced her first major manic episode. After several torturous and bizarre months, she ended up in a mental health treatment center in Las Vegas, New Mexico, where she was diagnosed with bipolar disorder.

There were more emotional and behavioral ups and downs, but eventually she stabilized enough to go back to college and earn a 4.0 GPA. She was about to graduate when, in the summer of 2002, she slipped into another devastating, four-month manic phase—which then cycled into an even more destructive depression in November and December.

On New Year's Eve, after Karla lapsed into a suicidal, catatonic state, Fran took her to a behavioral health care center in Tulsa, Oklahoma, where she was admitted. On January 10, the center released her against our wishes. Three days later, she found a hidden .22-caliber rifle, held it to her chest, pulled the trigger, and died instantly as the bullet ripped through her aorta. She was twenty-six, beautiful, intelligent, and charming, with a promising future. And she was dead.

Our grief remains profound. In the aftermath of her suicide and in memory of her, Fran, Kevin, and I did two specific things. First, we wrote a book, *The Tattered Tapestry,* describing our family's experience with Karla's bipolar illness, her suicide, and our own continuing grief.[1] Second, we formed the Karla Smith Foundation, whose mission is to "provide hope for a balanced life to family and friends of anyone with a mental illness or who lost a loved one to suicide." Its Web site is at www.karlasmithfoundation.org. In service of this mission, the Foundation teaches and promotes nine strategies for coping with the mental disorder of a loved one. These strategies emerged from our own experience of Karla's bipolar illness, the shared stories of others in similar situations, and our research through books, conferences, videos, and the Internet.

This book, *A Balanced Life,* is the result of our experience and research. Its nine chapters reflect the nine strategies. Each includes a commentary on that strategy, real-life stories of hope from those who have used it, and a series of questions for personal reflection and group discussion. Together, these strategies form the guiding material of the Karla Smith Foundation's support groups for the family and friends of a loved one with mental health problems.

What kinds of problems? In general, this book assumes that the person in question has a moderate to severe psychiatric disorder that is persistent or chronic. These people usually require ongoing long-term treatment and support from a network of people, including professionals, family and friends, and often the community. People with nonsevere disorders—such as milder forms of depression, anxiety, attention deficit disorder, and so on—usually need less intensive personal support; they can often lead independent, normal lives with medication, therapy, or both. Throughout this book, when we refer to mental illness, mental or psychiatric disorders, or mental health problems, we are talking about severe and chronic illnesses. And, although some mental disorders are apparent from birth, many of them emerge later, either gradually or suddenly, in childhood, adolescence, or adulthood. These later-onset disorders are the type primarily discussed in this book.

During the seven years my family struggled to cope with Karla's bipolar disorder, we received very little guidance. We had no coordinated response to her and no consistent advice on how to help her; no one attempted to understand or clarify our frustration, concern, and fear; we had no manual that suggested ways to cope with her mental problems. We did what we thought was the best for Karla, but we did it without confidence, and we regularly second-guessed ourselves.

We wish we had had these nine strategies to guide us while we tried to manage our responses to Karla and her disorder. We know that for every person with mental health problems, there are family members and friends who struggle as we did. We offer this book as a help to them, and we believe that living these strategies will bring balance, hope, and peace in troubled times.

...........Introduction

*Mental illnesses are shockingly common; they affect
almost every American family. It can happen to a
child, a brother, a grandparent, or a co-worker.
It can happen to someone from any background.
It can occur at any stage of life, from childhood
to old age. No community is unaffected by mental
illnesses; no school or workplace is untouched.*

. . . .

*In any given year, about 5% to 7% of
adults have a serious mental illness. . . . A
similar percentage of children—about 5% to
9%—have a serious emotional disturbance.
These figures mean that millions of adults and
children are disabled by mental illnesses every year.*

These startling statistics were revealed in a 2003 report, *Achieving the Promise: Transforming Mental Health Care in America,*

by the President's New Freedom Commission on Mental Health.[2] And each of these millions of people has a network of family and friends. If we assume at least four family members or close friends for each, then the number of people in the United States personally affected by mental illness is over 100 million.

Staggering as that number is, mental illness is experienced one person, one family, one friend at a time. While many symptoms are somewhat similar among people with the same general disorder, the individual stories of pain, confusion, frustration, and stigma are agonizingly personal.

Some people cope with their mental health problems quite well. They lead relatively balanced, productive, long lives and die of natural causes unrelated to their disorder. Other people suffer greatly, unable to control the extremes of their illness. They may limp from one major episode to another, they may live in a medicated haze, or they may create their own internal world severed from what most people consider reality.

Sometimes the mental illness ends in suicide. While suicides may involve a variety of factors—sociological, economic, and drug-related, among them—mental illness plays a part in many of them. The World Health Organization found in 2001 that suicide causes more deaths worldwide every year than homicide or war.[3]

But mental disorders can be managed, at least to some extent. Every situation is unique, but this is a fact for all people with a mental disorder: they can't manage the illness without some help. Left unchecked (which, in most cases, also means unmedicated), the illness will dominate a personality. The deterioration may be slow or rapid, but an untreated mental, behavioral, or emotional disorder will likely lead to increasingly pronounced erratic behavior—or at the very least, the condition will not improve. To control the illness, some type of treatment is necessary.

The nine strategies discussed here offer practical, humane ways to cope. While this book is written for the family and friends of a loved one with severe and persistent mental health problems, it could also directly benefit the person with the disorder, too. Ideally, that person might also read and discuss this book with friends and family to better understand their point of view—and to offer partnership with the strategies, if possible.

Balance

For people with a mental disorder and those who love them, the ultimate goal is recovery, which means balance. Anyone can strive for greater balance in life: that is a worthy goal. But most people without a mental illness already strike an acceptable level of emotional and behavioral balance somewhat automatically. Their body chemistry is relatively stable, and their emotional highs and lows stay within an expected range. Only at times of particular stress do these people feel a special need to rebalance their lives emotionally, mentally, spiritually, and behaviorally. And they regain that balance fairly easily, with medication, therapy, or simply with improved circumstances and time. For the most part, setting a goal to achieve a balanced life is not something they're especially motivated to do—there's no significant imbalance in their lives to recover from.

But for people with mental illness and those who love them, balance is not automatic. It must be achieved through conscious effort and planning, using effective strategies. And even when it is attained, balance does not mean the illness is cured. It means that it is contained, that the dangerous extremes of the disorder are usually in check. It means that the person can live a relatively peaceful and productive life with relationships that are stable and enriching, that the person can recover from a relapse with some confidence, and that the person's loved ones can enjoy a similar life.

With emotional, mental, spiritual, and behavioral balance, many people with mental disorders can experience life within the "normal" range of emotions, thoughts, and actions. They can manage in mainstream society without needing long-term institutionalization or withdrawal from life's daily challenges.

And these nine strategies can help strike and maintain that balance. Some people with severe brain damage or mental disability may not be able to comprehend the strategies, and they may need more specialized care. But for the millions who suffer from mood disorders, such as major depressive or bipolar disorders, these nine strategies, when reworded to apply directly to them, can provide a path to balance, productivity, healthy relationships, and peace. The same goes for many who suffer from schizophrenia, personality disorders, and anxiety or other disorders.

Mental disorders vary widely from person to person, and so do the solutions for managing them. Some of the strategies in this book may be most effective with particular types of illness, but much depends on the individual, too. The experience of a mental illness is unique to each person. Therefore, the path to a balanced life is different for each person traveling it. On the other hand, there are many common symptoms and experiences; indeed, this commonality makes it possible to formulate these nine strategies. The strategies can always be adapted to the particular situation at hand, as long as this is done within the strategies' general structure and spirit. Actively practicing all nine of them can greatly aid in achieving a balanced life for all concerned.

The Nine Strategies

Family and friends are often confused, angry, and frustrated by the behavior of their loved one. Even if counseling and treatment are underway, and family members have learned some basics about the illness, they may have no idea how to apply that knowledge: What can they do? How can they relate to the person? What should they be alert for? And how do they manage their own life balance in the process?

The nine strategies offer guidance on how to support the loved one and what to expect from him or her. Living with and responding to a person with a mental disorder often leads to emotional chaos. We may need to learn some new approaches. The relationship skills we've developed in "normal" settings over the course of our lives may not work as expected when we are relating in the chaotic world of mental illness. The rules are constantly changing, the dynamics of the relationship are volatile, and expectations are unanchored in everyday reality or common sense. Understandably, frustration is the result.

These strategies can bring some order to the chaos. They provide a framework for responding to the person with mental illness. They specify ways to provide advice and encouragement. They clarify expectations. They offer a systematic response to the question *What can I do?* And they are reliable,

The Nine Strategies

1. Help our loved one find and continue to take the medication needed for a balanced life.
2. Urge our loved one to maintain a supportive relationship with a therapist, counselor, or sponsor.
3. Learn as much as we can about the mental disorder of our loved one.
4. Assist our loved one in developing a healthy self-esteem, since it is critical for a balanced emotional life.
5. Accept mental illness as a fact of life for our loved one, even though this mental illness does not encompass all of life.
6. Take care of ourselves by proper exercise, sleep, diet, relationships, and by monitoring our feelings.
7. Become a supportive network of family and/or friends who know about the mental illness and who commit to acting in the best interest of our loved one as far as we are able.
8. Identify the early warning signs that precede a more difficult phase of the mental illness, and help our loved one when these signs emerge.
9. Acknowledge our dependence on a Higher Power and seek guidance from that Higher Power in whatever way that is comfortable to us.

since they are well grounded in experience and research; they are tested and proven.

As you apply these strategies on an ongoing basis, feel free to develop additional ones as needed. You may find that one of them has a particular aspect that warrants more attention. You might "spin off" that aspect into a tenth or eleventh strategy and focus even more consciously on it.

Whether you add to the list or not, consider these nine to be essential. Each one plays a specific role in helping manage the disorder, and to ignore any one of them could undermine all of them, maybe even dangerously. They are all about equal in importance, with strategy 1—medication—the absolutely pivotal one for most people. A person may be able to fudge slightly on the other strategies from time to time and avoid the extreme consequences of the illness. But not to stick with a properly prescribed and monitored medication plan is a sure path to disaster. With these strategies, by far the best approach is to accept and continually apply all nine. This commitment offers the greatest opportunity for ongoing emotionally balanced living.

A Long-Term Approach

Keep in mind the difference between a strategy and a tactic. A strategy is a plan of action designed to achieve a future outcome, usually for the long term. In the context of achieving balance with mental illness, these strategies anticipate significant change, and once implemented, they offer an ongoing improved way of thinking, feeling, and acting. A tactic, on the other hand, is a short-term action that produces a desired outcome. Strategies look to a future, more enduring result.

Coping

What do we mean by the term "coping"? We mean that we and our loved one are managing the impact of the illness well enough that we can live a reasonably peaceful life, and that the consequences of the illness do not interfere excessively with our daily living. Everyone has achieved an acceptable ongoing pattern of living. Everyone makes the necessary adjustments to relieve the burdens that living with mental illness can impose.

Coping does not mean the illness is cured. For the person with the disorder, coping means that it is controlled well enough to allow for extended times of reasonably peaceful living. For family and friends, coping means that even during ongoing difficult episodes or perhaps even disruptive psychotic behavior, they can remain relatively calm, helpful, concerned, and loving—but detached enough to continue their own lives. If there is a relapse into an extreme episode, everyone can return after intervention and treatment to an acceptable living pattern once again.

Coping is not a passive attitude. It is not something that happens *to* people; it requires consistent positive action. The strategies work for us only if we "work" them—if we use them actively. Working the nine strategies is anything but passive. We're not just memorizing them. We're applying them regularly. Reflecting, discussing, seeking implications, gaining insights from other people and resources, and discovering how the strategies impact us differently as the years go by—all these activities are implied in the term "coping." It takes work to cope. The nine strategies are guides to that work.

Mental Illness

Mental disorders take many forms. *The Diagnostic and Statistical Manual of Mental Disorders, Fourth Edition (DSM-IV),* published by the American Psychiatric Association, identifies hundreds of them. General classes of mental disorders include depressive disorders, bipolar disorders, anxiety disorders, eating disorders, personality disorders, and schizophrenia, among others. Each of these classes is divided into specific disorders. For example, according to the *DSM-IV,* the anxiety disorders class is divided into the following specific disorders: panic disorder without agoraphobia, panic disorder with agoraphobia, agoraphobia without history of panic disorder, specific phobia, social phobia, obsessive-compulsive disorder, post-traumatic stress disorder, acute stress disorder, generalized anxiety disorder, anxiety disorder due to a general medical condition, substance-induced anxiety disorder, and anxiety disorder not otherwise specified. (For more information on mental disorders, see appendix A.)

How many individuals with the various disorders described in the *DSM-IV* will respond to these nine strategies? It's hard to say. The first step is comprehension. To use the strategies, a person needs to understand their general meaning. If the mental illness prevents that, the strategies will be ineffective for that person. The second step is application. When someone does understand the core concepts, it becomes a matter of putting them to use—of living them. With those two steps, success is possible, and many disorders can be managed. The coping skills fostered by these nine strategies are not tailored to a particular mental illness; they are flexible enough to fit many situations.

What if the person with the disorder cannot or will not apply the strategies? The strategies can still have value for other people involved. Loved ones who follow the strategies can achieve some peace in their own lives, even as they relate to the person whose disorder is unmanaged. Coping with their loved one's frustration, anger, helplessness, and fear while showing patience and love is often a tremendous challenge for family members and friends. The nine strategies provide a road map to love without enabling, care without codependence, independence without abandonment, serenity without surrender, and order without controlling.

Try them and see if these strategies apply to your situation. They probably do—because they are flexible. They don't prescribe an exact solution; they help you organize your response to the disorder, and they provide a checklist of the major keys to coping with mental illness. Make a serious effort to use these strategies—and then decide whether they apply. Give them a good chance to work.

Group support is a big plus for families and friends, too. Find a group of people who are in situations like yours—ideally people who are also using or willing to use the nine strategies. Sharing your insights and experiences can be invaluable.

A mental disorder is not an automatic condemnation to a life of misery—either for the person diagnosed or for the family and friends. There is hope and opportunity for people with mental illness and those who love them. They can all live a balanced life, and these nine strategies will help.

Dual Diagnosis with Substance Abuse

In many cases, people with mental health problems also abuse or become addicted to alcohol or other drugs. This co-occurring disorder can complicate both diagnosis and treatment—of the mental illness as well as the substance use problem. (See appendix B for a more thorough discussion of substance abuse and dependence and how to respond.) The substance use may begin as a way to self-medicate the mental illness, an attempt to dull the emotional pain. However, for 8 to 10 percent of the general population, use can lead to abuse or dependence. In these cases, both the mental disorder and the substance use problem need to be addressed, preferably simultaneously in an integrated treatment program. And this "dual diagnosis" can mean even more confusion and frustration for everyone involved. How do we deal with both mental illness and addiction?

A dual approach can help us, too: we can get support for coping with both aspects of the problem. The nine strategies outlined in this book are consistent with the principles and practices of Al-Anon and Alateen, the Twelve Step programs that have been extremely helpful for the families and friends of alcoholics and addicts. Consider joining an Al-Anon support group as well as a mental health support group, as described above.

For the person with the dual diagnosis, Twelve Step groups such as Alcoholics Anonymous (AA), Narcotics Anonymous (NA), and Cocaine Anonymous (CA) offer invaluable support for recovery. These groups hold regular meetings—generally at least weekly, often daily. Many cities have multiple groups that meet in various locations. Some communities also have dual disorder support groups, such as Dual Recovery Anonymous (DRA).

Helping a Loved One

With these nine strategies, we are helping both ourselves and our loved one. Six of them call for us to take action that will directly improve our own coping abilities. And three of them—strategies 1, 2, and 4—speak of the need to *help, urge,* or *assist* the loved one. What does it mean to help, urge, or assist a person with a mental illness? It means to take an active role or even a proactive role in the care of the person, not waiting for him or her to ask for help. It means offering support emotionally, socially, spiritually, and intellectually. It means to advocate for your loved one when he or she is unable or unwilling to act in his or her own best interest.

And what about the term "loved one"? In some situations, family and friends don't always feel much love for the person with the diagnosis. At times, our frustration can so affect our feelings that it's hard to find the love anymore. Anger, disappointment, and powerlessness can override more positive feelings. These feelings of love and loss of love can come and go, and that is natural. So, for our purposes in this book, a "loved one" is anyone we have some responsibility for or care about personally. It may be a close family member or a friend. It can be a child, adolescent, or adult. It usually is someone we have known or lived with for a long time. A loved one is more than an acquaintance, a casual friend, or a co-worker sharing a job-based relationship. There is some level of commitment and responsibility for the person. We know that we will remain involved with the person even if, in our frustration, we sometimes feel like we want out of the situation.

We may not feel the love all the time. But as we learn more about the illness and work these nine strategies, we may find that we feel it more consistently.

STORIES OF Hope

What do these strategies look like in action? Each chapter in this book closes with several "stories of hope" based on actual life experiences. They tell about real people who have been through what we're going through—stories that may be hopeful, inspiring, tragic, or perhaps all of the above. They are all true in that they reflect the reality of loving a person with mental health problems. To protect anonymity, however, some of the names and details have been changed, and some are composite stories of people with similar experiences.

. . . .

QUESTIONS FOR GROUP DISCUSSION
OR PERSONAL REFLECTION

1. How much have you learned about mental illness in general?
2. How much do you know about the kinds of treatment and help available for a person with mental health problems? For the person's family and friends?
3. What does it mean to you to "lead a balanced life"?
4. How has living with a loved one with mental health problems created imbalance in your life?
5. Does your loved one have a dual diagnosis? If so, describe the relationship between the mental illness and the addiction.

6. Do you agree with the approach to "coping" described in this chapter? Do you believe that this level of coping is possible for you? Write down in what ways it is or isn't possible in your situation.

7. Outline the history of your loved one's mental health problems and the impact those problems have had on your family or friendship.

CHAPTER ONE

Medication

STRATEGY *1* *Help our loved one find and*
continue to take the medication
needed for a balanced life.

It sounds simple enough: take your medication. If you need medication for a balanced life, what could be more obvious? You get a prescription, then follow through and take it as indicated. It usually amounts to a pill or two, once or twice a day. People do it for all kinds of ailments, diseases, or pains. Many healthy people take pills to prevent illness, boost vitamin levels, reduce weight, strengthen bones, or replace hormones. Taking needed medications and supplements has become an everyday habit in our society, as common and natural as eating balanced meals.

Why, then, is taking their medication such an issue for so many people with mental health disorders?

It is, in fact, a serious problem. Getting the right prescription is the first hurdle. Thousands of people with mental illnesses don't have easy access to a professional who can prescribe medication; others are misdiagnosed and don't get the proper drug or the proper dose. But even with a correct diagnosis and the right prescription drug, some people may refuse to take it, forget to take it, stop taking it after starting it, fail to get refills in time, or adjust their own dosage without the guidance of their counselor or doctor. The consequences of any of these common behaviors is very likely to be a relapse into an unbalanced emotional state.

An outsider might judge these behaviors as foolish and irresponsible. The reality is more complicated, as we will see in our discussion of strategy 1.

The great majority of people with a severe, persistent mental disorder do need medication, usually in conjunction with counseling. Some may need medication initially until they are stabilized and able to take advantage of counseling—at which time they can reduce or discontinue their medication and resume it only if they have a relapse (a sequence of steps that must be supervised by a mental health professional). And in some less severe cases, balance may be achieved with counseling alone. But for most, medication is a key, ongoing necessity. Let's look at this crucial factor in more detail.

Finding the Medication

The challenges begin with the onset of the mental illness. While an early, quick, and accurate diagnosis of the disorder is obviously the best-case scenario, more often than not, signs of a mental health problem emerge slowly and with many confusing signals. Months, even years, may pass before the behavior reflecting a mental disorder leads to a diagnosis. In the meantime, the sufferer tries to understand and cope with thoughts, feelings, and behavior that stretch and then exceed the limits of normal. Family, friends, and co-workers, too, witness and experience this confusing struggle themselves. At this early stage, pinpointing a diagnosis—let alone the proper medication—is nearly impossible because the presenting symptoms are so complex and hard for everyone to interpret. Even doctors and other professionals may have trouble determining the exact nature of the disorder immediately. As a result, many people do not receive the medication they need as soon as they need it.

The complications can continue even after an accurate diagnosis is made. Choosing the right medication is not an exact science. Often, there are many drugs that are designed to control the symptoms of a specific disorder. Which one fits a given patient best? What factors lead a psychiatrist to prescribe a particular drug or combination of drugs for a patient? What dosage is needed? Many variables enter into those decisions: the intensity of the symptoms; the medications' side effects; the patient's personality, general health, and lifestyle; insurance plans and ability to pay; and so on.

Timing is another variable. Some drugs take weeks or months to make a noticeable difference—time that may be filled with discomfort and uncertainty. And even when an effective drug or combination of drugs is identified and taken consistently, there is no guarantee that it will remain effective forever. Eventually the patient's body chemistry may change, and the medication may lose its impact.

The side effects may create other physical or emotional problems as well. In response, the prescriber may adjust the dosage, switch to a new medication, or add a drug to counter the side effects. The jigsaw puzzle of factors may become more complex over time. It may seem that with each adjustment the cycle of cause and effect begins again, and more adjustments inevitably follow.

Finding the right medication is not simple, and the search seldom ends with the first choice. It may be a long process.

Finding Professional Help

Who will prescribe the medication? A psychiatrist or other mental health professional will need to choose it, prescribe it, and monitor it over time, preferably in an ongoing relationship with the client. Finding this person may also be difficult. How do we begin?

Everywhere in the United States, psychiatrists and other medical doctors can make a diagnosis and prescribe drugs. But beyond that, the professional credentials required to prescribe medications may vary from state to state. In some states, nurse practitioners can, too, and in a few states, Ph.D. psychologists can. Check with your counselor, social worker, or physician to find out your state's requirements.

Most counselors who can't prescribe meds are associated with a doctor or other professional who can, and they refer their clients to him or her for that purpose. Unfortunately, these specialists often have full schedules, and newly diagnosed people can wind up on waiting lists. If an episode reaches the level of possible suicide or other threat of harm, the person may be admitted to a hospital emergency room or treatment center. While in treatment, a person diagnosed with mental health problems will receive medication.

After the person leaves the facility, continuing access to medication becomes more problematic. For people with insurance, maintaining contact with the facility's doctor for meds is usually easier. For people without insurance, a variety of state-sponsored programs offer medication—but there is often a high turnover rate among the doctors who prescribe the meds. Doctor-patient relationships are often impersonal and short-term.

We live in a mobile society. If the patient tends to move often—as many college students and young adults do—finding the right professional help becomes even more complicated. And people with severe mental illnesses tend to lead more transient lives than the general population; some are estranged from their families. With each change of address comes the need to find a new person to prescribe the proper medication. And in this scenario, medical records often don't follow the patient in time for the new professional to study the medication history and weigh those factors in the balance. Besides, different professionals prefer different medications; their access to free samples of drugs may also differ. The counselor-patient relationship suffers, as does consistency in follow-through. Will the patient take the right meds in the right doses—or even take them at all?

How can family and friends help? They can

- help their loved one stabilize their living arrangements, if necessary
- find a reputable doctor or other mental health professional who can diagnose mental illnesses and prescribe meds
- help their loved one understand the dosage and side effects, and help devise a reminder system for taking the meds on schedule
- help their loved one handle any changes in meds and dosages over time. These adjustments are almost inevitable, and they can be frustrating, so emotional and practical support are helpful. The prescriber should also be kept up to date about the patient's response to the treatment.

What if the person denies having a mental disorder? Take the initiative and act independently: find a professional, discuss the problem, and together create a plan on how to approach the person's need for medication and other treatment. Meanwhile, you can join a support group for your own needs. Together with other people, you can seek ways to live with and love the person with mental health problems who won't accept help.

Staying on the Medication

The commitment to keep taking medication is as necessary as the initial commitment to begin taking it. Unfortunately, many people do quit their meds. Why?

Once stabilized, some people are lulled into thinking that they are now cured and no longer need to take their pills. As attractive as that idea is, it doesn't happen that way in practice. The medication is a major ongoing factor in their stabilization, and without it, the newfound balance is thrown off again.

Side effects are another reason. People usually experience some side effects, which vary depending on the medication. Some common side effects include nausea, tremors, weight gain, insomnia, loss of appetite, and a decrease in sexual desire. Some people become discouraged by the side effects and stop taking their meds. While many of these side effects can be uncomfortable, the consequences of dropping the medication will likely be much worse. But if the side effects are so debilitating that they actually are as bad as or worse than the illness itself, look for alternatives. Make an appointment with the mental health professional and keep searching for a medication that minimizes the side effects as it manages the mental disorder.

Other reasons people give for quitting their meds include difficulties getting refills, forgetfulness, inconvenience, and, with some drugs, the lowering of emotional "highs." While these reactions may be understandable, none of them is worth the consequences. Mental disorders are rooted in chemical imbalances, and medication is needed to right the balance. Medication is the keystone of the nine strategies: without it, the others may be ineffective. Let the motto "Take your meds" become your loved one's mantra.

Family and friends of a person with a mental disorder can play a crucial role in helping that person stay on the medication. There may be times when a loved one cannot make sound decisions, and family and friends have to make decisions for them. They need to know what the medication is, the correct dosage and frequency, where it is kept, how to get refills, what the side effects are, and whom to contact if necessary. They need to insist gently but firmly that their loved one must take it, and they need to monitor behavior so they can observe the impact of the drug.

In short, they need to be as informed about the medication as the person who takes it. They need permission from their loved one to have access to medical records, including medication information. The loved one may need to sign a document (usually available from a behavioral health care provider) that grants this access to a family member and/or trusted friend. Once this permission is granted, family and/or friends must talk to the doctor to learn about the medications and how they work. They must also know what signals to look for that might indicate that the drug is losing effectiveness or perhaps that the loved one has stopped taking it.

Above all, they must accept this reality: if the loved one has been diagnosed and prescribed a medication, it is absolutely necessary to take it. Even if the loved one argues against this need, even if the loved one becomes unstable, even if the loved one refuses to take the meds at a later time, family and friends must firmly, kindly, and patiently insist on continuing the medication.

To help prevent this potential conflict, it is wise for the family to discuss the "Take your meds no matter what" strategy with the loved one in advance, even when the loved one is in agreement with it. Being prepared emotionally and intellectually is the best way to handle the consequences of an unmedicated episode when it arises.

During a stable time, tell your loved one that you're committed to monitoring his or her meds, but that you don't want to nag. (There is a fine line between monitoring and nagging. Learn that difference.) You value independence and personal responsibility, but you know how essential this strategy is. You love them to the point of "meddling" in their lives for the sake of this strategy. It is more important that they continue their medication than it is for you not to meddle.

Ask your loved one to help plan ahead for this possibility. If the loved one refuses meds in the future, can you force the person to take them? Can you hide the meds in the person's food or drink until they stabilize again? Can you take the person to the emergency room or treatment center? Ask these questions and discuss these issues in advance. Establish a contingency plan so you don't have to make these decisions during a crisis.

Building a relationship based on trust and respect is essential for effective monitoring of medications; we will discuss this further in later chapters. For now, simply know that it is your vital role to do whatever it takes to help a loved one find the right medication and continue to take it as directed.

The Cost of Medication

Medication is expensive, especially measured over the course of a lifetime. Insurance covers some of it, provided the person is eligible and can afford the premiums. Even then, the co-pay cost is often a major budget item. At some point, family and friends may have to absorb some of the cost.

Many people with a mental disorder become eligible for state programs that include distribution of medication. Inpatient, outpatient, and disability programs offer consultation and medication free of charge, or for a minimal fee. But government funding for mental health is often a low priority for federal and state budgets. What patients need is a careful, ongoing analysis of their treatment options. What they often get instead are brief visits to an array of doctors, conflicting prescription philosophies, revolving medications, and continuing experimentation with new or different drugs. The professionals offering these services are often caring and conscientious, but they work in an underfunded and unreliable system.

Drug costs are a tangled problem for both the patient and the mental health system. Researching and developing new, more effective drugs is crucial but expensive. But the cost of *not* doing it is even greater in terms of human life and productivity—and even in dollar terms, when compared with the potential money saved over time by more effective, targeted medications.

Taking Medication Is Normal

Find the medication needed for a balanced life, take it, and keep taking it: this is the primary strategy that makes it possible to work on the other strategies. All nine can then coalesce into a program that makes a balanced life attainable for someone with a mental disorder, and for that person's family and friends.

Another way to say it is that taking medication is normal for a person with a mental disorder. People without a mental illness have a different "normal," one that does not involve these drugs.

But a mental disorder dictates a new normal, one that includes medication. For people who need insulin to control their diabetes, "normal" means taking insulin; likewise for people who need daily medication for their heart, blood pressure, or kidneys. Many people need medication to be normal. The same is true for people with mental disorders.

What is our message to our loved one who needs medication? One way to say it is this:

> *Take your meds. Always, take your meds. Don't second-guess your need to take your meds. Monitor your meds and the effect they have on you, but never stop taking them. Talk to your doctor about your meds, be open and honest with your family and friends about your meds and their impact on you, but take your meds. Never run out of your meds. Your meds make it possible for you to have a balanced life, so they are your most important medical strategy. There are no exceptions or substitutions: Take your meds.*

STORIES OF Hope

Staying on Meds

My twenty-six-year-old daughter was in a frightening manic phase of her bipolar disorder. Unknown to us, she had stopped taking her lithium months earlier, and now her world was full of bizarre fantasies, racing thoughts, unfathomable conversations, and dangerous relationships. Earlier, she had been generally faithful to taking her medication, saying she knew it was critical to maintaining balance in her life. She told us later that she had gradually stopped her lithium because of hand tremors, some weight gain, and her desire to feel "just a little manic." She felt she could monitor and manage her manic tendencies herself.

But it didn't work. She wound up struggling to re-register for her last semester in college, and I had joined her to help her find a new apartment and get settled. One night, she couldn't sleep. I was awake with her until midnight, visiting with some of her friends, but then she left around 2:00 a.m. to take a walk alone. She was gone all night. I was frantic. When she calmly strolled in at 7:00 a.m., she said she had a wonderful night and, by the way, this whole episode was being filmed remotely by her boyfriend in another state to be shown as a documentary on PBS.

She was scheduled to see her psychiatrist (who was out of town) in a few days, but I knew my daughter was in danger and I couldn't keep up with her. She needed medication. So I called her counselor, a wonderful woman who was very helpful to our whole family. The counselor and I arranged to meet at the local hospital emergency room with my daughter to begin the meds immediately. When we arrived at the hospital, my daughter protested taking one of them, but the counselor and I ultimately persuaded her to trust us and take it. It took some weeks, but with the medication, counseling, and family encouragement, she gradually came out of her manic phase.

The battle against her mental health problems was not over, but at that point, we made progress. We would still struggle to find the most effective combination of meds and dosages, but she never again experimented with quitting a prescription. I learned once again that I had a responsibility to do whatever I could to convince her to stay on her meds and to talk honestly with her psychiatrist about her compliance. Without medication, little else can be accomplished.

Finding the Right Meds

The struggle to find the right medication for our depressive son took years. The psychiatrist first put him on a low dose of an antidepressant, but it didn't seem to help him much. After a few months, the doctor upped the dosage, and our son began to come out of the depression. One of the side effects was nausea, and when it didn't go away after a few weeks, the psychiatrist switched him to another antidepressant.

The new medication seemed to work pretty well except for some side effects: our son couldn't sleep regularly, had some tremors, and complained about dry mouth. In time, he was feeling better despite the side effects, and he thought he could ease those effects by reducing his dosage. For the first month or so, he seemed to be doing okay. But then the depression came back, and it was very difficult to convince him to see the psychiatrist and his counselor about another medication change. Eventually he did get a different medication and, after experimenting with the dosage for a few months, the doctor found a combination of medication and dosage that let him function both at work and at home very well. That was about two years after his original diagnosis.

We finally felt that this piece of his treatment was in place. But unfortunately, three years later, he started slipping into another depression. First the doctor upped his dosage. But when that didn't have as strong an effect as we had hoped, he once again switched meds. This time it was a newer drug, and it did help enough to stabilize him.

After six years, our son is still functioning well, has a fine job, and is married with one child. He is committed to staying on his medication, his wife is very supportive, he sees his counselor regularly, and the future looks bright.

What we learned about medication in the past ten years is that the search for the right choice of drug and dosage takes a lot of patience and attention. Fortunately, our son eventually learned the same lesson. But we also learned not to be complacent. The drug may lose its effectiveness, or a serious side effect such as liver damage may emerge, or the person may decide he no longer needs to take it.

We are certainly grateful for our son's current state of mind, but we are always concerned that things may change. We know that it takes more than medication to live free of depressive symptoms. But the medication is a foundation. Without it, we feel his life, and therefore our own lives, would be more difficult and dangerous.

A Different Drummer

Little did my husband and I know what we were facing when we had our third child. We expected a normal childhood, but his was anything but. Today he'd be classified as ADD or ADHD—but back then they just called him a troublemaker. To us, he just always marched to a different drummer. As a baby he rocked and bumped his head in the crib so hard that it walked across the room; as a thirteen-year-old he used pot— he was always a little different from his siblings. In the 1970s, we were told that using pot was just like the beer drinking of our own teen years, but no one told us it would progress from pot to meth to crack.

Now, as an adult, our son has lost everything: wife, child, business. He lives with us and is trying to pull himself out of the hole he has dug. His daughter comes to visit and it is hard for her to understand the inevitable relapses. We have been through suicide threats and attempts. We have handled all his money as if he were a child; ultimately bankruptcy was unavoidable. Our son drifts from job to job, and even though he sees a counselor, it is still difficult for us to understand why he can't settle down and stay with one job. His dad and I are trying to be understanding and helpful, but our son needs to be a responsible adult and grow up. How are his problems linked together? Are the addictions rooted in his depression and hyper personality problems? We don't know.

At this point, he has finally stopped blaming us, at least openly, for all his problems. He is on Wellbutrin for depression, and that seems to have also stopped the urges to use. Will it help forever, or is this a stopgap? Is another relapse coming? It is hard not to be bitter, but it's also easy to love him. We want him to be like his siblings and be a responsible adult. We will not always be here, and his siblings' anger will be hard for him to overcome. We just pray that the medication continues to help him and that God will take care of him.

"I Just Want to Die"

I'll never forget the day my ten-year-old son came home from school, dropped his book bag, crawled under his bed, and announced, "My life is terrible; I just want to die." It broke my heart to see my intelligent, attractive, compassionate little boy feel so overwhelmed by his declining self-esteem, and his mounting social problems at school, that he was giving up on life at the ripe old age of ten. I tried everything I could think of to coax him out from under the bed—argument, logic, compassion, humor, ordering him out, offering a hug, a fun movie, even my ace in the hole—ice cream and cookies—but nothing worked. He had had enough, and now he just wanted to die. I tried joking with him and pulling on his legs to get him out. He clung tenaciously to the bed frame and I succeeded only in moving the bed with him underneath it.

The fact that his emotional pain was so debilitating was a bit less frightening to me, perhaps, because I had lived with it myself, and I could name it. At age ten, I had also begun a battle with depression—a battle that, despite my stubbornness, I could not win without medication. Clearly my son was now engaged in this same battle, and I did not want him to have to fight it alone for thirty years as I had. I knew my son needed my support, medicine to regulate his brain chemistry, and counseling to improve his self-esteem—in that order. But his most urgent need was to see some shred of hope and hold on to it until we could get in to see a psychiatrist and counselor.

With all of my other ideas and options exhausted that afternoon, I finally asked him what he wanted me to do. He said he wanted me to leave—he wanted to be alone. This seemed a bit of a risky option to me, but I could think of no others. I removed every sharp object from his room, closed the door, and gave him just a few minutes alone.

When I returned to his room, his window was open and he was gone. I panicked. Was he running to Main Street to throw himself in front of a car? Was he fleeing into the woods across the street in an effort to run away from his feelings? I ran around the house, calling for him, praying for the wisdom—or luck—to find him quickly. Before long, I caught sight of him in the yard, high up in a fir tree, where he had climbed to ensure his privacy. I kept watch on his position from the living room window, and I went out to meet him when he finally climbed down. (He was hungry.) Over a snack, we talked about what depression was, that it was an illness that made you feel really bad about yourself, and that much of what it made you feel was a lie—he was not stupid or worthless, but his brain chemistry made him feel that way.

It took three very long weeks before we could get in to see the psychiatrist. After taking the medication prescribed by the psychiatrist for a couple of weeks, my son began to feel much better. I felt blessed that he had been willing to listen to me, and to trust both me and his doctor to find a way out of those feelings of pain and hopelessness.

I felt equally blessed that the medication that had successfully restored my own brain chemistry also worked for his.

. . . .

QUESTIONS FOR GROUP DISCUSSION OR PERSONAL REFLECTION

1. Have you discussed the need for medication with your loved one? If so, what were the results of the conversation? If not, do you plan to initiate this discussion soon?
2. If your loved one needs medication for a mental disorder, has taking the medication been difficult for him or her? If so, how?
3. How do you see yourself as an advocate for your loved one?
4. At what stage did you receive an accurate diagnosis of the mental illness?
5. Does your loved one take an effective medication at this time? How is it helping?
6. What are the side effects of this medication?
7. What is your loved one's history with medication?
8. How do you describe your role in meeting and monitoring your loved one's medication needs?

9. What are your feelings about the mental health professional who prescribes this medication?

10. List your positive and negative experiences in the search for the "right" professional and the "right" medication.

11. To what extent has your loved one stayed on the medication? If he or she has quit taking it, what were the reasons? What were the consequences?

12. How do you handle the cost of the medication?

13. "Medication is the primary strategy for coping with mental disorders": what does this statement mean to you?

14. If you saw no way to convince your loved one to take medication—if the person denied having the disorder—what would you do?

CHAPTER TWO

Counseling

STRATEGY *2 Urge our loved one to maintain a supportive relationship with a therapist, counselor, or sponsor.*

This strategy is aimed at helping your loved one benefit from the talking and listening that professional counselors do. Counseling goes hand in hand with medication in treating the symptoms of mental illness. Sometimes the psychiatrist or other professional prescribing the medication also assumes the role of therapist or counselor. But more often, a counselor serves that purpose, meeting regularly with the client and also staying in touch with the prescriber to share information.

For our purposes here, the terms "therapist" and "counselor" are interchangeable. They both describe someone who has some educational credentials in psychology and who usually charges a fee to work with clients who are diagnosed with mental illness. The credentials could range from a masters or Ph.D. in social work, psychology, or other therapeutic discipline, to an M.D.

with a specialty in psychiatric counseling. The point is that the person has received formal training and is credentialed to provide therapy.

A sponsor, on the other hand, doesn't necessarily have a license or educational credentials—but ideally is someone who has gained valuable insight into mental health problems through experience and reflection. A sponsor volunteers to provide practical help and moral support for your loved one. Some organizations, such as Alcoholics Anonymous and Al-Anon, have a long-standing tradition of sponsorship, with guidelines for maximizing the success of the relationship. If your loved one has a co-occurring substance disorder, an AA or NA sponsor is an option, as is an Al-Anon sponsor for you.

Although there is no formal sponsorship network for people with mental disorders or their families and friends, such sponsors can be found, and it is well worth the effort. Even if you don't belong to a support group, you may find others who are in your situation and can offer advice and support: a friend, neighbor, or member of a religious congregation, for example.

Typically, a sponsor has experienced working or living with people with mental illnesses for some time and has achieved some level of insight and balance, regardless of the behavior of the loved one. Sponsors may also have a similar mental disorder themselves with some years of stability behind them. Sponsors are comfortable sharing their experience and insights with other people who have been in the same situation they've been in. Ideally, this person can become familiar with these nine strategies and work with your loved one using them as a guide.

But a sponsor generally does not take the place of a therapist for the person with the disorder. Along with proper medication, "talk therapy" is a process that has demonstrated its value in millions of cases. It often leads to greater self-understanding and acceptance—desirable goals for anyone, but particularly valuable for a person learning to manage the symptoms of a mental illness. Techniques vary, but the general purpose is to improve a person's ability to identify feelings accurately, express them appropriately, and accept them as a part of life. Another common goal is to forge new communication and behavior patterns. This means learning to recognize the thoughts and feelings that interfere with forming and sustaining meaningful relationships and otherwise living a productive life—and then to establish more effective patterns to replace them. This may take place in individual sessions or in group therapy, where a counselor facilitates this process among several clients sharing their thoughts and feelings.

There are other forms of therapy that don't emphasize verbal communication. These include art, music, and drama therapy; occupational therapy; physical therapy that provides release through exercise or sports; and various meditation methods. It is beyond our scope here to evaluate or recommend any of these techniques. That choice depends on the individual diagnosis and circumstances, with the family member or friend helping the loved one find the most helpful approach. Some studies have shown that, in the end, it is the quality of the relationship with the counselor that determines the therapy's success, as much as the method used.

Choosing a Therapist and a Sponsor

Ideally, a person with mental health problems has regular contact with a counselor and, if that counselor does not prescribe medications, also with a psychiatrist or someone else working hand in hand with the counselor. That team, along with a network of supportive family and friends—and a sponsor if one is available—provides the ideal combination of resources to create the best and safest environment. With this network, when one person isn't available, or is ineffective at the moment, another person can step in to fill the gap. (Chapter 7 offers a strategy for building such networks.)

This "best environment scenario" rarely falls into place automatically. One vital role for family and friends is to help build this support system. Together, they can search for the psychiatrist, therapist, and sponsor who best respond to the person's needs, since the person may not be able to conduct this search effectively or thoroughly alone. Part of "urging" a loved one to develop this ideal supportive situation is to do some research on mental health professionals and offer suggestions. And when these roles are in place, it's good for family and friends to know who these health care professionals are and generally how they work with the person. It is also wise to know their phone numbers and the dates and times of scheduled appointments. At some point it may be necessary to contact one or more of these people for advice or to let them know of any major changes in the person's behavior.

Counselors are not all the same. What factors go into choosing one? It's partly a matter of personal chemistry between counselor and client. Finding a counselor who is effective with your loved one can be a major task, involving some trial and error. A therapist may have an excellent reputation with positive references from many clients, but still may not be a good match for a particular client's personality and history. The search for a supportive counselor may take some time, considerable research, and lots of patience, but finding someone who gains the client's trust is worth all the effort. Such a therapist is a major benefit for all concerned.

Sometimes a client likes a counselor initially and makes progress with the therapy, but then begins to complain about the counselor. Family and friends need to be very careful at this point. Maybe the counselor is challenging the client to move ahead in dealing with some difficult or painful thoughts or feelings, ones that he or she would rather avoid. When this kind of resistance arises, the wisest approach for family and friends may be to support the counselor. If the client has granted disclosure rights to a family member or friend, that person needs to consult with the therapist. If these rights were not granted, family and friends are at a disadvantage. In any case, exercise care and cautious judgment when a loved one complains about a counselor. Sometimes, emotional and intellectual insights follow a period of resistance. If the client is able to make it through the resistance, the insight may be very helpful.

The Importance of Staying in Place

Once these supportive relationships are established, maintaining them is by far the best option. But what if the person with the disorder has the desire or opportunity to move to a different locale? Young people in particular, including college students, tend to change addresses regularly. But if the person has a mental disorder, the risks of moving are much higher. The onset of some disorders (bipolar, depression, and some anxiety illnesses, for example) often coincides with a young adult's desire or need to move. This combination of the onset of the disorder with a physical move can be devastating.

One of the biggest dangers of such transience is that it often severs the person's relationships with a support network, psychiatrist, counselor, family, friends, and sponsor. It becomes increasingly difficult to reestablish similar supportive relationships in a new locale. After a move (or two), the loved one may lose the motivation to search again for a new therapist or psychiatrist, which can lead to quitting meds, losing gains made in therapy, and eventually to a serious relapse into the worst symptoms of the illness.

It is up to family and friends to remind their loved one of the dangers of relocating. If a move is inevitable, then the family and friends can help arrange new relationships with mental health professionals who can provide medications and therapy—even if this arranging is done from a distance.

Building Communication Skills
Supports a Loved One's Therapy

Whatever is happening in the loved one's counseling sessions, family members and friends can support the person's progress in therapy and create stability in their own relationship by practicing effective communication skills.

Today, many people are seeking to improve their interpersonal communication skills, if the hundreds of books, articles, videos, and CDs on the subject are any indication. Let's review a few of the generally accepted principles of good interpersonal communication, as they are excellent tools for the family and friends of a person with mental health problems. Using these principles, even when the loved one does not reciprocate them, will help us keep our own life in balance.

In fact, counselors are likely to use these principles naturally in their own sessions with clients. If family and friends do the same, it helps present a unified approach to the person with the disorder. Using these principles helps set a calm, respectful tone that, over time, can help heal and stabilize even difficult relationships.

In his book *People Skills,* Robert Bolton discusses some of these principles in detail: listening skills, "I" messages, and three general qualities to cultivate: genuineness, nonpossessive love, and empathy.[4]

Listening Skills

ATTENDING SKILLS

Attending is giving your physical attention to another person, listening with your whole body. Attending is nonverbal communication. For example, nodding in agreement indicates that you are paying careful attention to the person who is talking.

FOLLOWING SKILLS

One of the listener's primary tasks is to stay out of the speaker's way so the speaker can say his or her piece. The listener is following, not leading; opening a door, not closing it. Some tools that aid this kind of communication are open questions, attentive silence, a nonintimidating invitation to talk, and brief indicators that the other person is being listened to attentively.

REFLECTIVE LISTENING

In a reflective response, the listener restates the content of what the speaker has communicated, and perhaps the feelings associated with it, in a way that demonstrates understanding and acceptance.

"I" Messages

When a person is hurt, disappointed, or upset, the "I" message technique can help keep the communication constructive. What's the difference between "I" and "you" messages? "You" messages can appear to be blaming, and may feel like an attack. As such, they may put the listener on the defensive, an immediate barrier to effective communication. With an "I" message, the speaker "owns" his or her feelings and opinions and states them straightforwardly. An "I" message can contain the word "you," but the main point is about the speaker. Some examples follow.

> **You message:** "You drive too fast! Are you trying to kill us?"
>
> **I message:** "When you drive fast, I'm upset because I'm afraid we're going to have an accident."

> **You message:** "You never hug me. I guess you don't love me anymore."
>
> **I message:** "When you don't hug me, it hurts because I'm afraid you don't love me."

> **You message:** "Turn your music down! You're so selfish—can't you see I'm trying to read?"
>
> **I message:** "When you turn the music up so high while I'm trying to read, I can't concentrate and I feel irritable.

> **You message:** "You're so undependable! You broke your promise to help me, just like you always do, and my plans are ruined."
>
> **I message:** "When you say you'll do something and then you don't do it, I'm disappointed because I based my plans on your help."

This "I" message approach has a three-part structure:

- a description of the behavior in question (the "When you . . ." part of the sentence)
- the speaker's feelings about it ("I'm upset" or "it hurts," for example)
- the specific effect (fear of an accident, inability to concentrate, and so on)

When you are upset—with the loved one or with anyone else—pause and frame your response as an "I" message. It may take practice, but this simple, proven technique can lead to much more meaningful communication.

Three Traits to Cultivate

Robert Bolton tells us that cultivating three particular qualities in oneself can also foster improved communication:

1. **Genuineness** means being honest and open about one's feelings, needs, and ideas.
2. **Nonpossessive love** involves accepting, respecting, and supporting another person in a nonpatronizing and freeing way.
3. **Empathy** refers to the ability to really see and hear other people and understand them from their perspective.

Roadblocks to Communication

But just as there are tried and true positive skills that support effective communication, there are also attitudes and actions that can interfere with it. Thomas Gordon lists some of these roadblocks in his book *Parent Effectiveness Training,* but they apply to any kind of relationship, not just those between parents and offspring.[5]

> **Criticizing:** Making negative evaluations of other people, their actions, or their attitudes. "You brought it on yourself! You've got nobody else to blame for the mess you are in."
>
> **Name-calling or labeling:** Putting down or stereotyping the other person. "What a dope!" "Isn't that just like a

woman?" "Dork!" "You rednecks are all alike." "That's exactly the kind of insensitivity I would expect from a man."

Diagnosing: Analyzing why people behave as they do; playing amateur psychiatrist. "I can read you like a book. You're obviously doing that just to irritate me." "Well, I think you're in denial about your anger."

Ordering: Commanding the other person to do something. "Take the garbage out right now—and I mean it!" "Why? Because I said so."

Threatening: Trying to control the other's actions by warning of negative consequences that you will instigate. "If you can't help out around the house, maybe I don't have to cook you supper every night."

Moralizing: Telling people what they *should* do; "preaching" at the other. "You shouldn't get a divorce; think of what will happen to the children." "You ought to tell him you are sorry."

Advising: Giving people solutions to their problems. "If I were you, I'd sure tell her off." "That's an easy one to solve. First I would . . ."

Diverting: Pushing the other's problems aside through distraction. "Don't dwell on it. Let's talk about something more pleasant." "Think you've got it bad? Let me tell you what happened to me."

Negating: Trying to stop people from feeling the negative emotions they are experiencing. "Don't worry—it's always darkest before the dawn." "It will all work out okay in the end."

These principles apply to any relationship and are widely known and supported by therapists and counselors. They can also help stabilize and nurture one's relationship with a loved one with mental health problems—even if they feel one-sided at times. Depending on the nature of the mental illness, the "normal" process of thinking, feeling, and acting may be replaced by delusions, emotional imbalance, and inappropriate behavior. As a result, many of these principles may not be immediately effective. The temptation at these times is to ignore these skills and perhaps revert to a more controlling stance. But that usually leads to more frustration, which adds even greater stress to the relationship. Even with a slow start, these principles can help heal and stabilize a difficult relationship.

Long experience teaches that active, reflective listening, using "I" messages, cultivating helpful traits, and avoiding roadblocks can greatly enhance communication, regardless of the loved one's ability to reciprocate. Nurturing the relationship often calls for greater patience and more attention to these communication techniques than usual. Consistency also helps. If most family members and friends understand and use these principles regularly, supportive and healthy relationships are more likely all around. Better communication takes practice, discipline, and commitment. A support group can help reinforce everyone's application of these principles.

But, for reasons of personal and societal safety, there may be occasions when family and friends need to use some form of power and control—perhaps "laying down the law" in a dangerous situation. If so, it is best to apply this authority with as much sensitivity and patience as possible. Anger and resentment only make matters worse. Even when pressed to use this power, family and friends can still use restraint, adhering to the techniques as closely as they can under the circumstances. Practice and commitment can help keep these skills active, even during an unusually difficult incident.

While there are many theories about and approaches to effective communication, the brief outline in this chapter is a reliable summary of the principles used by most mental health professionals. When family and friends also follow these principles, there is a united approach to the person with mental health problems. This united effort has the best chance of supporting the person most effectively—and that is why this part of this strategy is so critical. Counseling is essential, so family and friends should urge their loved one to maintain a supportive relationship with a psychiatrist and therapist. But they can also "practice what they urge": they, too, can use the communication skills promoted by the mental health professionals. This strategy helps to set a calm and respectful tone, which creates the stable, consistent environment that is conducive to a balanced life for all concerned.

STORIES OF Hope

"We Didn't Know What to Do"

When our son experienced his first major depression episode at age nineteen, we didn't know what to do. Our usual methods of encouragement and support— with some challenges and consequences when needed— didn't work. He simply stayed in bed and barely spoke.

We made some phone calls, got some references through the employee assistance program at my work-place, verified our insurance coverage, and contacted a counselor who seemed kind and knowledgeable. The counselor agreed to meet with our son and us. Since this was our first experience with counseling, we were all a little apprehensive, especially our son. The counselor met with him separately, and then with us. It was clear immediately that our son needed medication too, so the counselor helped schedule an appointment with a psychiatrist, who prescribed it.

The counseling was beneficial, even though our son said that at some of the sessions he was mostly silent. The counselor was sensitive enough not to push too hard when our son wasn't ready. In time, the sessions led to some valuable insights into our son's mental health problems and into our own efforts to cope with them.

We all learned from the counseling. As parents, we discovered what some of our own feelings were about— where they came from in our own personal histories. We also learned about our son's depression and how we could cope with it better. At first we were very cautious and worried about deciding what we could say to him and how to say it. But the counselor gave us some hints, and now we are better at being honest with our son. Our expectations for him have been modified by his mental illness, but we do still have some expectations. We expect him, for example, to take his medication, and we keep an eye on his compliance.

We don't see the counselor regularly anymore, but our son does. If we feel we need to schedule an appointment for ourselves, we will do so. In any case, our counselor has helped us immensely, and our lives are much better now.

Partnering with the Counselor

When our daughter went back to college after two years of battling the initial phases of her bipolar disorder, we all knew she needed a counselor. We called the university's counseling center and talked with the director of the department. After we outlined the recent history of our daughter's mental health problems, the director put us in touch with a counselor. Our daughter signed a waiver, permitting us to discuss her situation with the counselor.

This counselor proved to be a great asset in dealing with our daughter's illness, both for her and for us. Since our daughter had some previous counselors who were not very helpful—some of whom she really disliked—it was a relief and a blessing to have one who could relate to our daughter and us, and who obviously had a personal interest in all of us. As a result, our daughter made progress in her personal life and in school.

Improving Communication Skills

I had always thought that I was a good enough communicator. I never really had problems listening to others and saying what I wanted to say pretty clearly and with some sensitivity to the other person. I wasn't perfect by any means, but I certainly didn't think I needed to do anything special to improve my communication skills.

Then my husband started acting strangely. He became more and more withdrawn from me and from our two children. He lost interest in everything, even in sports. He went to work but came home exhausted and negative.

I got angry, and we had some heated quarrels. They felt one-sided, though, because he usually didn't even fight back—he just looked at me with blank eyes, making no effort to defend himself or explain what was going on within him. I became even more frustrated, afraid that I was losing my husband as a friend and that the children were losing their father.

Apparently something similar was happening at work, because his boss told him he had to see a doctor. Our medical doctor referred him to a psychiatrist, who ultimately diagnosed him as depressive and put him on an antidepressant. It took a month or so, but my husband gradually became less sad and more involved with us again.

For the most part, he remains responsive, but he is

not the same as he was before. I feel like I am living with a somewhat different person, and I struggle with how to relate and communicate with him.

During this whole time—about a year from his first symptoms until we leveled out somewhat—I learned some things about my communication skills. I was not as good at it as I'd thought. With the help of the counselor, I came to understand the importance of "I" messages and setting boundaries in my relationships, especially with my husband. After quite a few mistakes and feeling awkward about how to word my feelings (especially negative ones), I gradually became more comfortable with stating how I felt without putting guilt or expectations on him. He responded much better to this approach than I thought he would. It was surprisingly helpful. And while I am still adjusting to his mental health problems, I am better at talking with him, and our children, without getting too upset and angry.

I feel that my new ways of communicating are much more effective, and I intend to keep trying to improve. It also helps my husband better understand me and the impact of his illness on all of us. I know that without these new skills, I would never be able to cope with my husband's mental health problems.

· · · · · · · · · · ·

QUESTIONS FOR GROUP DISCUSSION OR PERSONAL REFLECTION

1. What is your opinion of the value of "talk therapy"?
2. Describe your experience with your loved one's therapist or counselor—and your own, if any.
3. This chapter refers to a "best environment scenario" for people with mental illness. How would you describe the best environment scenario for your loved one?

4. What is your role in terms of urging your loved one to maintain a supportive relationship with a counselor or sponsor?

5. What advantages might you gain by having a sponsor yourself? How might you go about finding a sponsor?

6. How well have you been able to communicate with your loved one?

7. To what extent are you familiar with the listening skills and the "I" message technique discussed in this chapter? Do you agree that these are useful skills and, if so, are you willing to commit to practicing them with your loved one?

8. Which of the roadblocks to communication do you identify with the most?

9. Have you ever had to exercise some one-sided control over your loved one for reasons of personal or societal safety? If so, in retrospect, could you have approached this situation differently? In what kinds of circumstances do you think using such power or control might be necessary?

CHAPTER THREE

Education

....

STRATEGY *3 Learn as much as we can about the mental disorder of our loved one.*

If someone we care about has a mental disorder, we already have some knowledge about that illness, probably based on our experience. But beyond that, what family members and friends know about their loved one's mental disorder can vary greatly. Minimally, they experience the person's behavior as unusual, beyond the scope of what they see in their other relationships. They may be able to identify some of the symptoms, sometimes very clearly and other times with less assurance. At this minimal level, they may not even know the name of the illness and may not understand the common symptoms in much detail. They are aware that "she is very depressed" or "he refuses to socialize with anyone." They know that "she has dramatic mood swings" or "he is just out of touch with reality." These symptoms throw their lives out of balance because their normal way of responding to people just doesn't work.

These observations are a good place to start, but it is wise to learn more—much more. More knowledge expands both our understanding and our coping abilities. And we don't need any special training or medical background to build our knowledge. Whatever our general level of education, this strategy offers guidance on how to educate ourselves on the mental disorder of our loved one so that we can use the other strategies to their best effect.

Educational Resources

Where do we start? There are a number of avenues for learning. If your loved one is seeing a psychiatrist and/or counselor, talk to those professionals about the disorder and ask for sources, either books or reliable Web sites, that discuss the illness. Once you have a diagnosis, you can narrow the field of research—but even without a diagnosis, professionals in the mental health field can recommend some reading to start with.

Books and Web sites are usually good starting points, but you'll also find magazine and journal articles, educational videos, TV documentaries, and movies on mental illness. In fact, you may be surprised by the sheer number of resources available. Again, ask the doctor or counselor to suggest material that would be most helpful for you. If you do this research on your own, look first for the simplest, most general description of the illness, its symptoms, and its treatment. And look for any references to the role of family and friends in treating the disorder.

Check for local support groups and local chapters of national organizations. All around the country, these groups provide information and emotional support for people with mental health problems and their family and friends. Consider these resources:

- **Depression and Bipolar Support Alliance (DBSA)** at www.dbsalliance.org. The mission of DBSA is to provide hope, help, and support to improve the lives of people living with depression or bipolar disorder. DBSA pursues and accomplishes this mission through peer-based, recovery-oriented, empowering services and resources.

- **National Alliance of Mental Illness (NAMI)** at www.nami.org. NAMI is the nation's largest grassroots organization for people with mental illnesses and their families. Founded in 1979, NAMI has affiliates in every state and in more than 1,100 local communities across the country. NAMI is dedicated to the eradication of mental illnesses and to the improvement of the quality of life for persons of all ages who are affected by mental illnesses.
- **Karla Smith Foundation (KSF)** at www.karlasmith foundation.org. As noted earlier, my wife and I, together with our son, started this foundation in memory of our daughter, Karla. KSF has an exclusive focus on family and friends of people with a mental illness. While it is not yet national in scope, it does offer educational resources and support groups designed to provide hope for a balanced life to family and friends of people with mental health problems.

Conferences and workshops are another resource. National organizations offer annual conferences and a variety of workshops, usually with tracks for families and friends, for consumers as well as health care professionals. State and county mental health agencies sponsor multiple programs for both professionals and the public. Check the Web sites of these mental health agencies for the most current information.

To be notified about upcoming events, have your name added to mailing lists that advertise them: ask the doctor, counselor, local hospital, or mental health treatment center to add you to those lists. You might also ask a leader in your religious community. Try universities, too: contact the psychology department, the department office for any health- and medicine-related fields, or the counseling department for information about programs.

Check newspapers and community calendars for items that announce these conferences, too.

Information or Misinformation?

How much information do we need about the mental disorder in order to understand and assist our loved one? On one end of the spectrum, there's the level of knowledge of a psychiatrist, psychologist, or behavioral research scientist. Obviously, that kind of knowledge is beyond most of us. On the other end of the spectrum, there are people we might call "underinformed": they have very little knowledge about mental illness or its treatment. Perhaps they know the name of the disorder, but that's about all.

But worse than being underinformed is being misinformed—or making superstitious or moralistic interpretations of mental disorders. For example, we still encounter the belief that all mental illness is the family's fault, that it's caused by the person's upbringing. This belief was especially widespread before scientific advances in genetics and neurochemistry showed the biological basis for most mental disorders. There are also people who still attribute mental illness to evil spirits or punishment by God for past sins. And many people are afraid of it: they think that all mentally ill people are dangerous, unpredictable, and to be avoided. Unfortunately, these false, superstitious beliefs have tended to stigmatize mental illness. This stigma still persists with some people; it is possible that a family member or friend of a person with mental health problems may believe some of this misinformation or superstition. In that case, basic, accurate, scientific information is needed to help the family member or friend change some of those erroneous beliefs.

So how much education does a supportive friend or family member need? We can aim for more than an "underinformed" level, but not so high as the "superinformed" professional level. We also need to rid ourselves of any taint of "misinformation" or prejudice about mental illness that we may have, even sub-consciously. Through no fault of our own, we may simply have absorbed the societal stigma more than we realize. So it is advisable that family and friends receive enough education to rid themselves of any false information about mental disorders. Without this basic level of reliable knowledge, we run the risk of making life even more unbalanced for our loved one and for ourselves. With false information, we can make matters worse, even when we are well-intentioned.

Each family member and friend will have to assess his or her own level of education honestly and seek the information needed to be comfortable with the subject. Only then can they truly understand, empathize, and help their loved one.

Overcoming Obstacles to Learning

Becoming educated about the mental illness of a loved one is not always easy, even when we are motivated to learn more. There are obstacles. Here are some common ones you may encounter:

The Information Is "Consumer-centric"

Within the mental health field, "consumer" is a common term for the person with the illness—that is, the client or patient. (Essentially, the person "consumes" mental health care services.) It is widely used to identify people with a mental illness without referring to a specific disorder. Family and friends might notice that most of the research, information, and educational material about mental illness centers on the consumer. Education specifically tailored to the family and friends is much more limited. Scientific research, for example, is almost exclusively focused on the consumer. This is understandable, but it may mean that families' and friends' needs are underserved. To know about the mental illness is one thing. To know what to do with that information in terms of relating to a loved one is another. It's this latter area that is often lacking.

The Information Is Too Technical

Much of the written material about mental illness is very technical in that it reflects discussions and research among professionals. For example, understanding the intended effects and the side effects of a medication can be bewildering. It's possible that a family member or friend who wants to learn more about a mental disorder can quickly be discouraged by the technical language used to describe the mental illness, its symptoms, and its treatments. It doesn't take long to feel overwhelmed by the task of learning about a field we have not been prepared for and don't have the educational background to understand.

Our Own Commitment May Be Lacking

This obstacle may be hard to recognize at first, but identifying it may be an essential key to our learning. If we are truly committed to learning more and have a deep desire to be better informed, we will find a way to become more educated. But are we really that committed? Do we view our education as an ongoing process? We may want easy answers, guaranteed solutions, a clear diagnosis, and even clearer directions on how to cope with our loved one. When we do not quickly find these answers, solutions, and directions, we give up the search for more knowledge about the mental illness. Especially if we become frustrated and bewildered, it can seem that it just isn't worth the effort to learn more.

The Illness Baffles Us

The illness itself may leave us feeling totally puzzled and confounded. Compared to the common signs of "physical" illnesses—such as fever, localized pain, or fatigue—the symptoms of mental disorders are more behavioral; they also tend to be more unpredictable. When symptomatic behavior is erratic, and especially when it's disruptive or harmful, it can be hard to tell where the illness begins and personal responsibility stops. The line between illness and responsibility can appear to shift, so we don't know whether to blame the illness or the person. In frustration, we may throw up our hands and give up trying to learn more about the illness.

We Rely Too Heavily on Our Loved One

Do we count on our loved one to provide whatever we need to know about the illness? If so, we're getting all our information secondhand and filtered through his or her perceptions. We need more objective information about the nature, symptoms, and treatment of the disorder. We certainly shouldn't dismiss the testimony of our loved one about the illness. In fact, that testimony is extremely valuable. But relying exclusively on our loved one to educate us can leave us poorly informed.

One or more of these obstacles may apply to you, and there may be others. But whatever they are, they can be overcome. The first step is to identify them and name them accurately. Drawing from the five obstacles mentioned here, or others that you notice, list your own personal barriers to learning more about the mental illness of your loved one. Address each issue separately and adopt a plan to counteract each obstacle. Take it slowly, at a pace that feels comfortable. There is no need to try to learn everything immediately. Use the resources mentioned on pages 46 and 47 to get started.

The critical factor is our desire to learn. The truth is that greater knowledge of the illness will help us relate better to our loved one. Without some level of understanding, we will not know what is happening to our loved one, and we may hold impossible expectations that can only cause conflicts and long-term frustration. Knowledge can help us better interpret what is happening. With accurate knowledge of the cause, symptoms, and treatment of the illness, we will understand better, and our relationship will improve.

Education: Limits and Possibilities

Of course, there will be limits to our knowledge about the mental illness of our loved one. We are not psychiatrists. But we can go well beyond the basics. It is essential that we learn the basics early on: common symptoms, medication needs, a general diagnostic plan, and treatment options. In fact, our initial confrontation with mental illness usually prompts some education right away. Then, over time, many people tend to learn in spurts, on an as-needed basis. As the illness progresses, we often learn more, usually as a result of some further crisis. This is experience-driven education. When the experience no longer changes significantly, we tend to stop exploring and learning.

But it is wise to learn at times other than a crisis. This ongoing education can prepare us for an uncertain future, and it also puts us in a better position to help other people in a situation like ours. Such outreach is essential in a society where there is such misinformation and stigma associated with mental illness. Knowledgeable family and friends can become effective advocates for people with mental disorders, especially those who cannot speak for themselves. It is better to push our limits in the direction of greater knowledge and not to be satisfied with a minimal understanding.

There are also limits to what our education can accomplish in itself. Knowledge alone doesn't cure the illness or totally resolve our difficulties in coping with our loved one. We may be perfectly aware of how to solve a problem, but we don't necessarily act to solve it. Many smokers, for example, admit that smoking is bad, but they do not stop smoking. Advice from doctors about dieting, exercise, drinking, sleeping, and medication is often ignored even though people agree that it is good advice. Knowledge alone doesn't guarantee solutions or necessarily lead to positive behavioral changes.

Education may have its limitations, but it is an important link in the chain. All nine strategies are vital for coping with the mental illness of a loved one. All nine contribute to a plan for relating to our loved one. Knowledge is not an instant cure-all, but it can help in far-reaching ways. Each strategy, including education, is an important piece of developing the ability to cope with the mental illness.

Education for Society

In July 2003, the President's Commission on Mental Health is-sued its final report, *Achieving the Promise: Transforming Mental Health Care in America.* The first goal in a transformed mental health system, the Commission insisted, is that "Americans un-derstand that mental health is essential to overall health." This understanding is "fundamental for establishing a health system that treats mental illnesses with the same urgency as it treats physical illnesses." To help achieve this goal, the Commission made two recommendations:

1. Advance and implement a national campaign to reduce the stigma of seeking care and a national strategy for suicide prevention.
2. Address mental health with the same urgency as physical health.[6]

Research shows that the most effective way to reduce stigma is through personal contact with someone with a mental illness. Family and friends can help transform this societal stigma into acceptance and understanding. We are often afraid to speak about our experience with mental illness to our friends, co-workers, acquaintances, or other groups. We may think that it is a private matter to be kept within our families or that some physical, social, or economic harm will come to our loved one or ourselves.

There is, of course, a need to protect confidentiality and respect privacy. On the other hand, when more families and friends of people with mental disorders do share their experi-ence, knowledge, love, and understanding with other people and society in general, the stigma will decrease. The result will encourage more people to come forward and seek professional help when needed. Widespread disclosure of mental illness, told in countless personal stories, will improve mental health care in our country.

In the long run, this strategy is essential not only on a personal level as we cope with the mental illness of our loved one, but on a societal level, where mental illness needs to be acknowledged and addressed far more effectively.

STORIES OF Hope
....

Support Group Learning

When we first went to a support group for the family and friends of someone with mental health problems, we didn't know what to expect. Our daughter was twenty-five and had been recently diagnosed with schizophrenia. We were scared and confused, and we didn't know very much about the illness.

The group was helpful, and it was comforting to know that other people were in the same situation. But we still needed to know more about schizophrenia and how our daughter and we could cope with it. Through the support group, we learned about the National Alliance on Mental Illness (NAMI) and its "Family to Family" program.

One night a week for twelve weeks we attended this course, which covered a good number of mental disorders and included handouts at each session. At the end of the course, we each had a large three-ring binder filled with information not only on schizophrenia and other brain disorders, but also on medication, communication skills, advocacy, and viewpoints from people with mental illnesses themselves. The course gave us a broad introduction to our daughter's schizophrenia and answered many of our questions about the disorder.

Our new knowledge doesn't take away the difficulties of coping with her illness, but we now understand better what is going on with her. We know what to expect and are not as surprised by her behavior. We still have to deal with her illness, but we are much more confident in our approach to her now.

Learning by Mistakes

I still don't know when my husband's behavior crossed the line. He had always been the life of the party, and his reputation as a comic and a great storyteller was part of what attracted me to him. We both enjoyed going out on Friday and Saturday nights to party, drink, and have fun with anyone who would join us.

At some point, his joking and stories became more exaggerated, and I knew that what he was saying was not what he had experienced. His fantasies about his accomplishments at work, in sports, or in life in general were simply not true—not even close. His plans for the future, like building a NASCAR racetrack on some farmland my parents owned, were totally unrealistic and impossible.

I love my husband, and we have always been able to talk openly about things, so I asked him about some of these fantasies and plans. He expanded on his ideas with me in private, and after a while, I became very concerned and suggested that he see his doctor. He objected at first, but eventually he agreed. Some time later, after a number of visits with his doctor and then a psychiatrist, he was diagnosed as bipolar.

I wasn't really shocked by the diagnosis because I knew something was wrong, and it was a relief to have a name for it. But I didn't know what it meant to have bipolar disorder. My husband accepted the diagnosis much better than I thought he would, and he shared with me a lot of what he learned and said in his therapy sessions. Over time, I learned about his mental illness mainly by talking to him. He sounded like he was becoming an authority on his own illness.

The next few years went by rather calmly. He took his medication faithfully, and we stopped partying so often. Our lifestyle became calmer, and it seemed like we could manage his illness quite well.

But then my husband started telling me that his counselor said that he could gradually stop taking his medication. Bipolar disorder was something that he could get over, he said. It was a temporary illness that many people, after taking the medication for a few years, could overcome—and then they could stop taking the meds. He had gained some weight and was worried about possible liver damage, both common side effects of the medication.

He was very convincing, and I believed him immediately. I, too, wanted his illness to end. My husband quit his medication, but without the supervision of his prescriber.

Within three months, his old fantasies returned, and he got into an argument with my parents about the farmland and his plans to build a racetrack. I asked my husband to go back to his counselor. When he said that wasn't necessary, I pleaded with him. He still refused, and when, after a while, he became depressed, I contacted his counselor myself—and learned that she had never advised him to quit his meds.

Eventually, he did realize that he needed help. He went back to his counselor and is now taking his medication again. He will probably need it for the rest of his life, and we both understand that now.

But this time, I was determined to learn about his illness from someone other than my husband. I read some books, did research on the Internet, joined a support group for families and friends of people with mental health problems, and talked with some counselors myself. I realized that I made a mistake by relying on my husband to tell me about his illness. We still talk about it openly, and I believe him most of the time. But I now have some objective information that helps me confirm whether his perceptions of his disorder fit the general knowledge I have. When we disagree on how to interpret a symptom, handle a side effect, or start a plan of action, we ask his counselor or psychiatrist. This approach works much better for me—and for my husband. There is no substitute for accurate information about mental illness.

"Someone We No Longer Recognized"

It was her junior year of high school, and our daughter's behavior had become more and more troubling. Growing up, she had always been considerate, practical, and mindful of the reasons behind the rules of our household. But over the past two years, she had become someone we no longer recognized. Our home lives were filled with unwelcome drama—rude, angry, resentful behavior toward us; an insistence that the rules didn't matter, or didn't apply to her anyway; increasingly risky behaviors that only made her life more miserable; frequent, unpredictable bouts of emotional hysterics for no apparent reason; and, finally, suicide attempts.

I knew my daughter was suffering from depression—the same illness that I had fought, and my mother before me, and her mother before her. But she was certainly struggling with even more than that—and what it was, I had no idea. It was terrifying to watch her sink deeper and deeper into hopelessness, unwilling to listen to anything we said, unable to recognize that she was causing so much of her own distress, and blaming everything on us all the while. Her doctor referred us to a counselor and, much to my relief, she agreed to go. But after only a few sessions, she abandoned the effort, apparently unwilling to honestly examine her emotions and her situation.

The counselor shared with me that she was very concerned about my daughter, who seemed to be developing borderline personality disorder. I had never heard of this illness, and as she described the symptoms, I was not only surprised to see that such a variety of problems all belonged to the same disorder, but also dismayed to recognize nearly every symptom in her behavior.

Although my daughter refused any more visits to the counselor, I continued to see her for several more sessions. As a mom, I naturally felt at least somewhat responsible for the poor and dangerous choices my daughter was making. My self-confidence was plummeting in the face of what seemed to me (and to many people outside of the situation) to be a parenting disaster. The counselor reassured me that I was doing fine as a parent, and that our home life was not causing the disorder. She was able to recommend several excellent books, answer my questions about the illness, support me and help me work through the challenges of parenting a teen with this disorder, and help me keep everything in its proper perspective. I was able to understand my daughter's thoughts and feelings more clearly, and to separate who she really was (the child I loved) from the symptoms of her illness (which I hated). I also learned to distinguish what I could and should do for her from what she could only do for herself.

I couldn't force her to get counseling for herself, but my continued sessions certainly helped me set my course and stay strong in the face of the many struggles that lay ahead. And that was a real benefit to our entire family, including my daughter.

· · · · · · · · · · ·

QUESTIONS FOR GROUP DISCUSSION
OR PERSONAL REFLECTION

1. On a scale of 1 to 5, with 1 being very little and 5 being a lot, how much would you say you know about the mental disorder of your loved one?
2. How did you come to learn about the disorder? What sources of information did you use?
3. Have you ever attended a conference or workshop on the disorder? If so, what did you learn?
4. What were some of the erroneous beliefs you had about mental illness before your loved one's disorder prompted you to learn more?
5. How important is it to you that all close family members and friends have a similar level of knowledge about the mental illness?
6. Of the five common obstacles to education listed in this chapter, which ones describe your situation?
7. Describe your own level of desire to learn more about the mental illness of your loved one.
8. To what extent has your learning been "experience-driven," prompted by your desire to understand and relate better to your loved one? To what extent has it been driven by a desire to learn more about the illness?
9. If it is hard for you to share your experience of your loved one's disorder with other people, what might be the reasons for that difficulty?

CHAPTER FOUR Self-Esteem
. . . .

STRATEGY *4 Assist our loved one in*
developing a healthy self-
esteem, since it is critical
for a balanced life.

The dictionary definition of "self-esteem" is helpful, but not complete: "belief in oneself; self-respect." For the verb "esteem" we find "to set a value on, whether high or low; to estimate; to value." Under "self-esteem," one thesaurus adds terms such as "self-worth, confidence, sense of worth." These definitions do capture the common understanding of the term, and in this chapter we will build on that understanding. Although various branches of psychology have developed many theories and insights related to the concept, we need not survey them here. Our purpose here is to explore ways to assist our loved one in developing and sustaining a healthy self-esteem.

What is a healthy self-esteem? It is a balanced one, neither too low nor too high, one that reflects an accurate and realistic opinion of one's self. A healthy self-esteem boosts a person's ability to function appropriately in a family and in society. Generally, self-esteem develops over a lifetime and, under normal circumstances, the experiences of childhood and adolescence provide the time and setting for this development.

A Balanced View of One's Self

Even people without mental illness don't always have a positive view of themselves. Some people seem to navigate the tides of self-esteem quite easily, handling some natural ups and downs in self-image with no trouble. But other people struggle for years, and perhaps a lifetime, always swimming against the tide and never truly overcoming their low self-regard. Their thoughts may reflect this negative self-image: *I'm not worth very much; I don't measure up; Other people are always better than me;* and *I often mess things up.* This view could come from a number of sources: a childhood environment that reinforced these negative messages, a tendency to find self-value by comparing oneself to others, or a traumatic experience that led to a pervasive, deep-seated guilt.

It seems evident that most people have experienced at least a temporary period of low self-esteem at some point in their lives. They have an occasional spell of feeling bad about themselves, but then, after time, counseling, or personal reflection, they regain a more positive view.

Psychological research and our own personal experience attest to the importance of a positive view of oneself. Self-esteem emerges as one of the critical pillars of a healthy personality. Without it, a balanced life is extremely difficult. With it, people are able to respond appropriately to the joys and sorrows of life and remain relatively confident and happy.

Self-Esteem and Mental Illness

Building and sustaining genuine self-esteem is an ongoing struggle for people with a mental illness. By nature, debilitating disorders such as depression, anxiety, and the delusional systems of schizophrenia or bipolar disorders can undermine people's best efforts. For most people, self-esteem is directly related to meeting certain basic needs: satisfying relationships with family and peers, a lasting intimate partnership, and meaningful work. Success in these key areas reinforces a positive self-image. But that success may feel elusive to a person with a mental illness—and self-esteem can be seriously compromised, especially if the illness is serious and persistent.

A mentally ill person's emotions can seem like a river run wild. One's feelings can seem as unpredictable as cascading down white-water rapids in a small rubber raft without oars, crashing dangerously among jagged boulders, dropping unexpectedly down frightening waterfalls, spinning uncontrollably in eddies and whirlpools, never knowing when the chaos will end. The self-image of a person with a mental disorder is usually battered by negative thoughts, feelings of unworthiness, dread of others' expectations, and the sense of being a burden to the world, to their loved ones, and to themselves.

In the end, though, no matter what the challenges, each of us—whether we have a mental illness or not—is responsible for our own self-esteem. While family and friends can help establish a climate in which self-esteem is not further damaged, and can support the person's sense of self-worth, this is something that has to eventually come from within that person. Even people with chronic mental disorders can cultivate a positive sense of self. By taking their medications, going regularly to their therapist and/or support groups, accepting the help and care of family and friends, and having realistic goals, they can find value in their lives.

What Family and Friends Can Do

This strategy has two parts: minimizing the negative self-image, and maximizing the positive. Family and friends can assist their loved one by (1) avoiding any words or actions that may feed a negative self-image and (2) creating a climate of acceptance, open-ness, and respect—an atmosphere of unconditional love. Neither of these offers guaranteed results. But applying this strategy consistently over time will offer a loved one a good chance for a positive self-image, as reflected through your genuine caring and appreciative feedback. At the least, family and friends who use this strategy can be assured that they aren't contributing to their loved one's negative self-regard.

Loving a person with mental illness often takes lots of effort and patience. In normal relationships, we expect occasional conflicts, anger, frustration, or disappointment. People often say negative and hurtful things to one another. The same is true when we relate to someone with a mental illness, with the added challenge of trying to discern when the person's behavior might stem from the illness itself. While not excusing unacceptable behavior, family and friends will be more helpful if they learn how to separate symptomatic behavior from irresponsible behavior and, in either case, try to respond patiently, avoiding negative judgments and accusations. This takes practice and commitment. We are learning how to be patient and understanding—while also holding firm, clear, reasonable expectations that respect our loved one's capacity to take responsibility. Patience and understanding are desirable in all relationships, but especially so when mental illness is involved. Use those skills and everyone will reap the benefits.

Can self-esteem be too positive? Some forms of mental illness may include an exaggerated, unrealistically positive self-esteem—the manic phase of bipolar disorder, for example. People in this phase often believe they can accomplish more than their skills or circumstances will allow. They lack the healthy critical self-awareness we all need to help us know our limitations. While it is always important to support the dreams and good intentions of a person with mental illness, it is equally important to help the person distinguish between achievable dreams and destructive fantasies. In these cases, family and friends try to gently bring their loved one to a more reasonable view of their limitations.

Unconditional love lies at the heart of helping a loved one with mental health issues develop positive self-esteem. But as a society, we are geared toward conditional love: in overt and subtle ways, we learn how to love on the condition that someone else's behavior and attitudes meet our expectations.

The delicate line between necessary, healthy expectations and conditional love is hard to identify and even more complicated to apply effectively. Parents, for example, generally expect that their children will meet certain behavioral, educational, and social standards. At the same time, they strive to love their children unconditionally. It's common to hear adults recalling their own childhood and testifying to their parents' failure to separate their expressions of love from their performance or behavior expectations for the child. We don't always learn unconditional love at home.

Through adolescence and into adulthood, we may not experience unconditional love, either. Competition in school, in the workplace, in sports, in social circles, and even in entertainment and arts all contribute to a society that constantly compares. Someone is "better" (which means someone else is "worse"); someone wins while others lose; some people presumably succeed and others fail. This message is everywhere—in popular media, in advertising, and in our language. We are expected to behave, think, and feel in particular ways, or be shunned, minimized, ignored, or condemned.

The stigma against mental illness thrives in this environment, unfortunately. This atmosphere also doesn't promote learning how to love unconditionally. But loving unconditionally is one of the most important things that family and friends of people with mental illness can learn to do.

How do we do this? Maintain a positive attitude. Compliment your loved one often. Avoid making comparisons. Don't take the person's insults, disrespect, anger, and rejection too personally. Make a habit of showing that you genuinely care about their well-being. Wish them well in all their endeavors, help them achieve appropriate goals, listen to them closely, and try to understand the world from their perspective. To love unconditionally means to care for, respect, understand, and forgive another person regardless of their response to your efforts. "Regardless" is the hard part. Loving a person with mental health problems requires a commitment to this kind of love, even as we know that we will sometimes fail.

Societal Stigma against Mental Illness

Through our relationships, we can help boost a loved one's self-esteem. But let's look briefly at the societal context in which these relationships are formed. The stigma against mental illness is real, even though in the past few decades there has been some improvement in the general social acceptance and understanding of it. As the President's Commission on Mental Health described it in its 2003 report entitled *Achieving the Promise:*

> Stigma refers to a cluster of negative attitudes and beliefs that motivate the general public to fear, reject, avoid, and discriminate against people with mental illnesses. Stigma is widespread in the United States and other Western nations. Stigma leads others to avoid living, socializing, or working with, renting to, or employing people with mental disorders, such as schizophrenia. It leads to low self-esteem, isolation, and hopelessness. It deters the public from seeking and wanting to pay for care. Responding to stigma, people with mental health problems internalize public attitudes and become so embarrassed or ashamed that they often conceal symptoms and fail to seek treatment.[7]

As someone close to a person with mental health problems, you probably know about this stigma all too well. To help counter it, we can, both by example and education, foster neighborhoods and communities that accept people for who they are rather than judge them by false societal measures of success. People with physical disabilities seem to be gaining more acceptability in society than people with mental illness are. Perhaps the celebrity testimonials, public service advertising campaigns, and school programs that have eased the stigma for physical disabilities can do the same for mental illness. Many of these activities can be instigated and led by family and friends.

A healthy self-esteem is essential to a balanced life, and this strategy is worth lots of time, discussion, and effort. Self-esteem is an immeasurable asset to people with mental illness. It can be the emotional anchor that allows them to monitor their medication, use counseling effectively, regulate their schedule, know their strengths and limits, and seek and accept help when needed. Family and friends are in a position to help with this development, since they are in regular contact. They know their loved one's personality, thought patterns, habits, preferences, and feelings. Practicing unconditional love, they can create a supportive environment where their loved one has the best chance of experiencing the benefits of a healthy self-esteem.

STORIES OF Hope
. . . .

Unconditional Love

I don't know which came first, the alcoholism or the anxiety. But at age forty-eight, my son was in the throes of both. He has been in treatment four times in his life and is now sober and taking his medication. I am grateful for today, but I have no illusions about how long this calm state will last. My experience with him over the years keeps me cautious about predicting the future.

My husband and I have spent years trying to figure out the best way to support and love our son. We tried "tough love," but when we were convinced that his suicide or death by alcohol in the streets was a real probability, we took him back into our home and helped him with a job. We tried "soft love" by listening to him for hours and giving him all the physical and emotional support we could muster. He has good intentions, goes to AA, and tries to keep sober, but eventually he relapses and quickly becomes consumed by the alcohol and the depression.

He lost his marriage long ago but loves his daughter, who is now married and lives in a different state. His siblings support him in general, but they don't know what else to do to help him. He lost his driver's license because of a number of DUIs. He now lives alone and is barely able to keep up the house payments because of his irregular attendance at work. He is a very kind man, but his anxiety—which leads to depression— seems to weigh him down even when he is on his meds and sober.

I worry about him often. Our other six children are doing relatively well in life and relationships. I sometimes wondered what I did wrong with him, but I am now less hard on myself and see that my husband and I are not the cause of his illness and alcoholism. To a large extent, our son is not the cause either. I see his problems more as an illness, like diabetes or cancer, than as a behavioral issue or a character defect.

But it wasn't always that way. There were years when I felt he was totally responsible for his drinking, and I sometimes blamed him. I never directly accused him, but I felt that way, and felt guilty about feeling that way. A counselor friend of mine helped him and me understand his situation better, and even when he relapses now, he comes back a little faster. I fear we may still find him dead on the street some night from alcoholism, but I am grateful that he is alive today and somewhat happy.

Throughout all these years of struggle, I was aware that his self-esteem was very low. I have tried to encourage him and point out his strengths to him and to others, but I don't think it really helped him that much. What my husband and I have come to believe is that we need to love our son unconditionally as best we can. We don't always know what that kind of love means practically and in specific situations, but it's what we strive to do. We have heard of unconditional love all our lives, especially in church, but our situation with our son makes it very real and personal.

What we have learned is that in order to love unconditionally we have to ask ourselves regularly if we can identify any conditions on our love for our son. Conditional love can sneak in very easily. Of course we need to set healthy, legitimate boundaries with him. But we have to know the difference between maintaining those boundaries and placing conditions on our love. We don't have a foolproof formula for identifying that difference, but we try. At this point, the best we can do is to try, and to hope that our decisions reflect our unconditional love.

We cannot fix our son. His depression and alcoholism are his demons, and in the final analysis, he has to do what he can to contain them. What we can do as his parents is to offer an atmosphere of steady acceptance and a constant message that we love him, in the hope that he will respond positively. That's what we pray for and try to achieve.

The Stigma of Mental Illness

I believe the stigma of mental disorders is preventing my family from facing the reality of my daughter's illness. The symptoms of her bizarre behavior began about a year ago, when she was twenty-one. After an initial outburst of energy and drastically changed behavior, she fell into a depression. She wouldn't come out of her room and would barely eat. She didn't want any help, and she kept telling us that nothing was wrong and to leave her alone. When I suggested that she might be depressed and that she needed to see a counselor, she became very angry and told me that she was not "nuts" and certainly was not going to see a shrink. She didn't want to be labeled "crazy" for the rest of her life, and if her friends found out, they would pull away from her and tell others that she was acting weird. There was no way she was going to face them if they thought she was a lunatic. She just wanted to be left alone.

When I talked to my husband about her, he thought I was overreacting. In his view, she was going through a phase, something related to growing up, and she would be back on track in time. He thought I might be alarmed because I didn't want to face the fact that she was becoming an adult. It was also clear that he didn't want me to tell anyone else about our daughter's struggle. I should leave her alone, and he would handle it. I knew he meant that he would do nothing and would get along with our daughter by agreeing with everything she said and did.

Over the next few months, she became even more reclusive and lost a dangerous amount of weight. Things got so bad that even my husband agreed that she needed to go to the hospital. There was a lot of difficulty getting her admitted, but eventually she went in for assessment. Since there was some previous drug use in her history, the doctors couldn't be sure of her diagnosis, but they were convinced that her behavior warranted some kind of treatment.

Even after this hospital visit and a follow-up appointment with a counselor and a psychiatrist, my daughter and my husband seemed more concerned about who might find out about this "episode" than about the seriousness of her illness. To them, it still was not a mental illness. I believe their denial is mostly caused by the stigma associated with mental health issues. I know how they feel, because I had similar feelings when her problems first emerged. But I now see that her mental health is much more important than what other people think about her. I am determined not to let the stigma interfere with the help my daughter needs. My next step in overcoming this stigma is to convince my daughter and my husband to accept the reality and the seriousness of her situation.

. . . .

QUESTIONS FOR GROUP DISCUSSION OR PERSONAL REFLECTION

1. How do you describe "self-esteem"?
2. Give some examples of people who, in your opinion, have a healthy self-esteem.
3. Give some examples of people who, in your opinion, lack a healthy self-esteem.
4. Name some ways in which mental illness may have undermined your loved one's self-esteem.
5. Name some ways in which a positive view of oneself can contribute to a healthy, balanced personality. How have you experienced this?
6. To what extent is each person responsible for his or her own self-esteem? Is this level of responsibility the same for a person with mental health problems? If not, how does it differ?
7. To what extent do other people contribute to an individual's self-esteem? Is that extent the same in relation to people with mental illness?
8. This chapter compares the struggle for a healthy self-esteem for someone with mental health problems to trying to navigate a river run wild. In what ways does that describe the struggle of your loved one for self-esteem?

9. The text mentions two general ways to help your loved one develop self-esteem: (1) Avoid words or actions that may feed a negative self-image, and (2) Create a climate of acceptance, openness, and respect—an atmosphere of unconditional love. How have you been able to put these into practice with your loved one? What are your obstacles to practicing them?

10. How have you managed to balance unconditional love with necessary, healthy expectations and boundaries? What have been obstacles in achieving this balance?

11. How have you experienced unconditional love yourself?

12. The quote from *Achieving the Promise* describes the negative impact of stigma. In what ways have you experienced this stigma? What can you do to help erase it?

CHAPTER FIVE
.... Acceptance

STRATEGY *5* *Accept mental illness as a*
fact of life for our loved one, even
though this mental illness does not
encompass all of life.

Acceptance of a mental illness is difficult for all concerned. It is hard because it brings us face to face with something we did not ask for, something we cannot banish with a magic pill or by simply trying harder. For those with the disorder, and those close to them, "working the strategies" in this book can moderate the negative effects of mental illness and allow for a relatively balanced life. And in some cases, such as some mood disorders, there are periods of remission when life returns to normal. But in most cases, a chronic mental illness is like a chronic physical disease such as diabetes or Crohn's disease: the person who has it generally will have to learn to manage it for life, and family and friends will have to adjust their lives to accommodate the disruptions it causes as well.

Why Is Acceptance So Hard?

For many of us, the idea of acceptance implies that we must admit our limitations, and most of us resist this. We are comfortable enough with some limitations: we usually can accept that we will never run a four-minute mile, write the great American novel, or learn calculus in a day. But other limitations we may not accept so easily, especially in areas of our life where we think we have more control than we do. At times, most of us would like to control what other people think, feel, and do. But over and over again we discover that people have their own ideas about what they should do. And they may behave unpredictably, simply ignoring what we think they "should" do. We eventually realize that we have little control over others or, in fact, over many circumstances in life.

Acceptance can be difficult because it forces us to deal with reality—a slippery concept. What is real and what is illusion? Whose reality are we talking about? What is the concrete, definitive truth of our life, and what is a fantasy, naïve expectation, or unrealistic wish? These questions are not just for philosophers, poets, and pundits. In the special circumstances we live in, we all face these questions every day. We seldom ask them directly, but we often think, feel, and act as if we know the answers when, in fact, we don't.

When we do assess our real abilities and limitations honestly and critically, we often see that we have less control than we thought. A sudden illness, an unexpected death, the unwanted end of a relationship, a child growing up and resisting our guidance, a person who makes a choice we don't approve of, a loved one in trouble who refuses our help, a friend who disappoints us, a decision we make that has unforeseen painful consequences— all these real-life experiences expose our own limits and vulnerabilities. And we don't like it.

Acceptance in such situations is difficult because it means we have to honestly acknowledge unwanted limitations; it means we choose to think, feel, and act within those restrictions. It often takes a long time to learn how and when to accept these life realities. Some people never really learn this kind of acceptance, and few people, if any, practice it all the time. Most of us have to work at it, and now and then we slip back into our old patterns, trying to control people and circumstances that are beyond our control. Learning to accept our real limitations gracefully can be a lifelong lesson.

Healthy acceptance doesn't mean being passive in the face of life's difficulties. It isn't giving up or escapism. It doesn't mean repressing our frustration and inwardly "rolling our eyes" when things don't go our way. True acceptance only rarely comes after a hard-fought, stubborn face-off with reality. Instead, it usually comes over time, as we develop a more mature response to the things we truly have no control over. Eventually, healthy acceptance is quiet, clear-eyed, determined, and kind. And the reward for this high level of acceptance is greater personal peace and more congenial, relaxed relationships—which make life easier, more enjoyable, and more productive.

Acceptance and Mental Illness

For family and friends of people with mental health problems, learning acceptance is a pivotal issue. When faced with our loved one's unusual thought patterns and behavior, our first response— out of our own fear, embarrassment, and genuine concern—may be to try to shape his or her thoughts and behavior, to "normalize" the situation. The tendency to try to control and change our loved one's symptomatic behavior is very strong.

This tendency is complicated by the fact that when our loved ones *are* more in control of their thoughts and feelings, we *can* have some impact on their behavior; they are as responsive as anyone is to others' needs and expectations. But, as we asked earlier, where is the line between what our loved ones can do freely and voluntarily, and what their illness compels them to do? What are they responsible for and what is caused by the illness? Since it's impossible to draw a clear, fixed line between these two realities, we struggle with our role as caregivers. The influence we have is real and can be beneficial, but there are areas where we have no influence, even if we want it and they want it. That's when acceptance becomes essential.

Mental Illness Is Experienced Uniquely

No two people are exactly alike, and no two people experience a mental illness identically. Each disorder, even with its specific diagnostic symptoms that are consistent from person to person, feels different and is expressed differently by every one of those people. The differences may be dramatic, as various as their personalities themselves. As a result, family and friends must adjust what they've learned about the illness to their loved one's own situation. Nobody's experience goes strictly "by the book." When figuring out our expectations, we need to factor in those individualities.

Similarly, we all will express and practice acceptance at different levels and in unique ways. Some of us may relate successfully with most other people in our lives but can't connect very well with the person with mental health problems. Others might find it relatively easy to relate to the same loved one. Or there may be a particular behavior that one person has a hard time accepting, while others don't have a problem with it at all.

Acceptance, then, is an individual experience. While family and friends can guide and encourage each other to learn acceptance, it is ultimately an individual, personal responsibility.

Accepting the reality of a mental illness is difficult, period. When a newborn enters a family, there are hopes and expectations for that infant. We look forward to the growth of the child, with visions of who and what that child will become. None of those hopes and expectations includes the disruption and pain of mental illness. Friends who knew the loved one before the onset of the illness will have to completely revise their needs and expectations for their friendship. Sometimes the symptoms of the disorder emerge gradually, sometimes abruptly. In any case, when the illness first appears, we are bewildered, frustrated, and often angry. Our loved one's behavior can be unpredictable, incomprehensible, and frightening— perhaps especially before a correct diagnosis is made, which can take years in some extreme cases. Denial is usually part of that early reaction. We typically don't immediately think of mental illness as the cause of a loved one's problems, mainly because we would rather it be anything but that. We search for other explanations of the behavior, often blaming the loved one, or even ourselves, for what we think are character defects, irresponsibility, or bad choices.

With other illnesses, from the flu to cancer, we can usually get a definitive diagnosis rather quickly. As bad as the news might be, there's some comfort in knowing the cause of the problem. And it is usually quickly followed by some clear treatment options—we know what we have to do. With mental illness, we often don't know the cause of the problem for a long time. As a result, acceptance may be impossible in those early stages, because we don't really know what we're dealing with.

But even after we get an accurate diagnosis from a professional, we tend to deny or minimize the problem. We don't want to believe it. The stigma of mental illness prevents many of us from fully accepting this reality, and we would rather believe that our loved one is an exception, even when the symptoms are definitive. It can't be "that bad." We want to believe that the right medication will regulate the illness and, for all practical purposes, neutralize the symptoms; everything will return to "normal." We often deny the full impact of the illness on our loved one and on ourselves.

In short, we fight acceptance because we just don't want to live with mental illness. We weren't prepared for it and don't want to change our lives because of it. We long for the illness to stop tormenting our loved one. We try to adjust to this upheaval in our lives, but we don't know how. Whether this initial denial is conscious or not, it is perfectly understandable. Acceptance usually comes gradually. Often we can accept the illness intellectually before we do emotionally. It takes time to accept the consequences emotionally and, over the long haul, this acceptance can be elusive—it comes and goes, with some periods of peace and other times of great turmoil.

If we work on acceptance, think about it, talk about it, and share our feelings about it, we can eventually arrive at a more or less permanent state of emotional acceptance. It's especially helpful when we see other family and friends experience it. Their witness is inspiring, and their journey is worthy of imitation. Their stories may not exactly match our own, but there will be enough similarity to show us how to find our own path to acceptance and peace. Even though it seems impossible at times, acceptance can be a reality for all of us.

There's More to Our Loved Ones Than Their Mental Illness

Another important insight can help us apply this strategy of acceptance: our loved one's mental illness does not entirely define who they are—or who we are. As we go through the difficult process of acknowledging the reality of the mental illness, we may tend to view our loved one exclusively in light of that illness. That tendency is reasonable. Our loved one's thoughts and behavior can be so dominated by the symptoms, demanding so much of our time and energy, that other qualities of that person and our relationship with him or her can shrink to insignificance. In fact, we may pay so much attention to the illness—the symptoms, the medication, and the treatment—that we and our loved one may start to believe that nothing else matters. This reaction is so common that it is predictable, particularly in the early stages of learning to cope.

Since we know the person best and care most deeply, family and friends are in a unique position to help our loved one keep a healthy perspective on the disorder. The psychiatrist, counselor, or sponsor will necessarily focus on the illness; that is their role with your loved one. And there are certainly times when we also have to focus on their illness. But it is crucial that we don't let the mental illness define our loved one—or us—and that we pay attention to and celebrate other aspects of our lives together. We can still enjoy our normal routines with our loved one: sharing meals, watching TV, going to movies or concerts, visiting friends, pursuing hobbies, attending religious services, shopping, playing sports and games, and so on. We can still talk and laugh and cry together as we find the connections that have always been there and that can sustain a loving relationship. Life with our loved one doesn't have to be one long therapy session. In fact, the best therapy for everyone may be to relate to each other as much as possible without any reference to the mental illness.

It is also healthy for family and friends to maintain a life apart from the person with the disorder. Work, other friendships, hobbies and interests not related to our loved one—these also need our time and attention. In particular, parents of a child with mental illness need to create time away from their child. This need is so great that the next strategy we'll discuss, self-care, concentrates on this issue alone. Here we emphasize that mental illness, even as demanding, time-consuming, and emotionally draining as it is, does not and must not dominate our lives.

Finally, even if we find the right medication and counselor, learn everything there is to know about our loved one's mental illness, and nurture the person's self-esteem, without mental and emotional acceptance of the disorder, our lives will continue to be in turmoil. Ongoing denial, minimizing, rejection, and other habits of avoidance will lead to anger, alienation, and unnecessary frustration. Besides, without acceptance, we cannot give fully to our loved one. With acceptance, we experience personal peace, and we provide the best support we can. By consciously accepting our loved one's mental illness while not letting this completely define our relationship, we can embrace all aspects of our lives together. And we can begin to restore balance for our loved ones and for ourselves.

From Frustration to Acceptance

When our daughter was diagnosed with borderline personality disorder at age nine, we were not surprised. We didn't know much about this disorder, but we did know that her behavior called for some special attention. She did well enough in her schoolwork, but she did not socialize very well with other kids—or with anyone. Upon advice from some psychiatrists, we enrolled her in a boarding school for borderline children, where she did quite well until she was twelve. At that point, she transferred to a local school.

She did fine in high school academically, but she had no friends and didn't seem interested in making any. She was confrontational with us and most other people, but it didn't seem to bother her. Typical of those with borderline personality disorder, she denied she had any problems and blamed other people for any difficulties she experienced.

We were embarrassed for her because we knew that her antisocial behavior gave her a reputation of being aloof, selfish, and hard to get along with. That kind of behavior was just the opposite of our own ways of relating, and the contrast was surprising and, frankly, disappointing. We were constantly frustrated as we tried to influence her behavior over all these years, but we were not able to effect much change in her.

After she graduated from high school, she bounced around from job to job, usually waitressing. Each time, it wouldn't be long before she decided she didn't like her employers or some other circumstance about the place, and she quit. According to her, the problem was always with other people, and she was totally innocent.

She also spent money frivolously and expected us to pay for everything. She is our daughter and we love her, but the clash between her personality disorder and our own way of life is obvious and deep-seated.

Our daughter is now over thirty years old and living in another state. She seems to be doing better. There really is no medication for borderline personality disorder that deals directly with the causes. Some medications can address some of the symptoms, but she will not take anything because she doesn't believe she really has a problem. She will never view relationships or life the way we do, but it now appears that she will probably get by on her own terms and in her own way. She seems to have adapted just enough to make this possible.

For us, our journey with her has led from continual frustration to acceptance. We are now better able to detach ourselves from the consequences of her behavior. It helps that she is no longer a child and that society holds her more accountable for what she does, and not us. Living in another state also means that she does not expect us to bail her out whenever her behavior gets her into trouble.

Somewhere along the way, we learned how to accept her and her disorder. We cannot change her, but we can still love her.

"I Just Wanted to Help My Sister"

When my sister went into an extremely manic phase of her bipolar disorder, I decided to be as supportive and helpful to her as I could. After three years of relative stability, she had gradually taken herself off her lithium and, before long, was in a seriously psychotic state. I was in another city, so I couldn't be with her physically. But I was determined to see her through this difficult period and get her restabilized.

Since my sister couldn't focus on anything but her fantasies at this time, I decided I would keep a log, recording how her behavior affected me and other people. My idea was to help her see how her manic thinking and actions looked from my perspective, which I knew was very different from her own.

I wrote the chronology for about three months. Every time I talked with my sister, or with other people about her, I recorded the basics of the conversation. As I went from day to day, I became even more aware of the extremes of her illness. I had followed her in previous depressions and manic episodes, but never this closely and intensely. Some days it was hard to believe what she was doing and how she was thinking. And there was no way to predict what she would do the next day. But I was committed to helping her as best I could and to recording each day's events.

I stopped the chronology when it appeared that my sister was finally coming down from the mania. I was exhausted. Along with other members of the family and some friends, I finally got her to see a doctor and get some medication. A few weeks later she started to improve, and it seemed like the end of this long, dangerous, taxing, and nerve-wracking manic time was in sight.

My sister wasn't aware that I had been writing the chronology, so I flew into town to see her and gave it to her. She was clearly more balanced, but still recovering from the mania. She accepted the lengthy document and thanked me for doing it, but she wasn't yet able to deal with the content of the chronology. I knew it was too much for her at that time, but I hoped that in the future she would read it more objectively, and then she and I could talk about it.

One of the things I learned by this very close, intense relationship with her, and by recording those events, is that the illness has a destructive life of its own. I could do very little to stop it or change it. And I learned that she couldn't stop it or change it either. Only the medication could put her in a position to reach some stability. I had hoped it was otherwise, that I could protect her from some of the impact of her mania. Maybe I did, but for the most part, I had to accept the limitations of my ability to help her. I loved her throughout this whole ordeal, but love alone does not cure mental illness.

I now know better what acceptance means. Being such a close witness to a major mental health problem taught me that it is valuable to do whatever I can to help a person or a situation, but that in the end, it is also important to accept what I cannot change.

. . . .

QUESTIONS FOR GROUP DISCUSSION OR PERSONAL REFLECTION

1. Describe some areas in your life, other than coping with the mental illness of your loved one, where you have had to accept your limitations.
2. Based on your experiences with your loved one's mental illness, how would you define acceptance?
3. How has acceptance been rewarding for you?
4. Have you noticed that you've tended to try to control your loved one's behavior? If so, what has been the outcome?
5. Were there times when you were in denial about the mental illness of your loved one? When you minimized the impact of the illness? What other defenses have you used as barriers to accepting your loved one's mental illness?
6. How do you develop your relationship with your loved one in ways that have nothing to do with the mental illness?

CHAPTER SIX

.... # Self-Care

STRATEGY *6* *Take care of ourselves by proper exercise, sleep, diet, relationships, and by monitoring our feelings.*

The cost of relating to and caring for a loved one with mental health problems is often high. Financially, thousands of dollars may be spent on doctors, counselors, prescriptions, treatment, and unusual living expenses. But the emotional and personal costs may be even higher.

Of course, we want the best for our loved ones. We want to do what we can to help them experience life as fully and joyfully as possible. As those closest to them, we are willing to make sacrifices and adjustments for them, even though we know that gratitude—from them and from others—may be in short supply.

The kind of unrelenting commitment that is often required takes so much extra intellectual, physical, and emotional energy and time, that we simply get worn out. The social and even spiritual drain can also be tremendous. Loving a person with mental illness is a massive challenge, and it quickly upsets the balance of our lives.

That's why it is essential that we take care of ourselves while we take care of our loved one. Everyone needs to eat healthy foods, exercise regularly, sleep well, and maintain positive relationships to maintain an optimum quality of life. But these standard, commonsense recommendations have added urgency for the family and friends of a loved one with mental health problems. Because we can become so focused on meeting our loved one's needs, we can easily forget to take care of ourselves. This sixth strategy—self-care—is vital for creating balance in our own lives, because by ignoring it, we make it all but impossible to practice the other strategies effectively.

Proper Exercise, Sleep, and Diet

These three components of a healthy lifestyle are extra important when we are meeting the challenges of caring for a loved one with mental health problems. Many programs and approaches are available that promote healthy habits and techniques for exercise, sleep, and diet: books, videos, and so on. But experts in all three of these fields advise us to establish a consistent daily routine that incorporates these disciplines into our lives, not as added chores or occasional pursuits to be done only when convenient. A regular routine of self-care will best prepare us to deal with the inevitable stress of learning to cope with the mental illness of a loved one.

By taking proper care of ourselves, we are affirming our own worth. We are also practicing the principle, discussed earlier, of relating to our loved one, and others, in "non-illness-centered" ways—focusing on other issues as well. And we are modeling self-care for our loved ones, who, because of their illness, may neglect their own physical health and hygiene. Many studies have shown that proper nutrition, sufficient sleep, and regular aerobic exercise help stabilize and even lessen the severity of many of the symptoms of mental illness, not to mention what physical well-being does for our outlook on life and self-esteem.

Other Relationships

For a balanced life, it is vital that we develop and maintain relationships with people who are not associated with our loved one. These relationships provide us with much-needed emotional support and the sustenance of receiving as much as we give. They also help us see beyond our loved one's mental illness by expanding our focus in the world. Co-workers, people who share a common interest with us, old friends, neighbors, people in our religious congregation or other groups we belong to—all can help fulfill our emotional and social needs outside of the world of our loved one's mental illness. They are vital to a balanced life.

At another level, we need to look at our closer relationships, particularly those with the network of family and friends that we share with our loved one. The trouble is, it's easy to let our relationship with our loved one become the center of our life. It may happen gradually and without a conscious decision, but we can easily end up spending much of our time and emotional energy there, and neglecting other family members and intimate friends. A person with a mental illness demands more attention, time, and energy than a normal relationship does. We are left trying to choose between devoting additional care to our loved one and giving normal attention to other relationships. We try not to neglect these relationships, but when that happens, we presume and hope that these people will understand and adjust their needs accordingly. We begin to divide our attention differently.

In some networks of families and friends, this "balance of attention" may shift without much trouble. When everyone in the network understands and accepts the imbalance and adjusts willingly, there is less chance of resentment, neglect, and tension.

But often these shifts in attention are not acknowledged or talked about, and they do cause problems. Some people in the network may be conscious of the imbalance—they see that the person with the disorder is occupying more of a particular persons' time and attention—but they feel it's too delicate to discuss. Or perhaps they feel so guilty that they don't talk about it, even though they may resent the imbalance. Sometimes, spouses, families, and friends don't identify their anger and resentment accurately, and they end up just being angry in general. In any case, in coping with a loved one's mental illness, everyone in the system of relationships will have to adjust in some way.

Facing this issue together, directly and honestly, is a form of self-care, the point of this strategy. Ignoring our concerns is the worst-case scenario for self-care. For balance in our relationships, it is essential that the network of family and friends talk about all their relationships in the context of the loved one with mental health problems. Everyone needs a common understanding of how they will relate to their loved one and among themselves. Everyone needs to be "on the same page." For everyone's sake, it is important that the family doesn't take one approach and friends take a different approach to the mental illness of the loved one.

Since this network typically consists of up to ten people and sometimes many more, the intertwining relationships are complex. Some of us see the person with the disorder often and are very close; some less so. The same is true of our relations to others within the network: it's unlikely that we all connect equally with each other. In the next chapter, we will examine more closely how a network with these complex dynamics can support the person with mental illness.

Monitoring Our Feelings

We know how essential it is to talk about resentment and other negative feelings that arise as we struggle with caring for our loved one. But sometimes talk is not enough: we need a plan of

action. If you, or anyone, feels resentful, the following suggestions may help defuse it. Each person can choose how to express these feelings, and to whom. The point is for the feelings
to be identified, expressed, and acknowledged compassionately
by others.

- Admit the resentment to other people in the network but
  not, at this point, to the person with the disorder. It is
  an understandable emotion in these circumstances, and
  denying it or being defensive about it isn't necessary or
  helpful. Other people in the network need to accept the
  resentment with compassion, even if they don't share it.
  The listening skills and "I" messages outlined in chapter 2 are helpful in these situations. The point here is to
  admit and state the resentment to people who accept and
  understand the feeling.
- List the reasons for your resentment. What's behind it?
  Discuss these reasons with other members of the network; learn how they handle similar situations. See a
  counselor; join a support group; learn more about the
  illness—seek the roots of your own resentment.
- Claim the resentment. We own our feelings: no one can
  make us feel anything. Other people and circumstances
  are occasions for us to react in a particular way, but they
  don't create our feelings—our feelings come from within
  ourselves. It isn't helpful or accurate to blame the person
  with the disorder for our feelings of resentment.
- Let go of the resentment. Since we own these feelings,
  we alone can change them. Hanging on to them will
  only hurt ourselves and interfere with our other relationships. Letting go implies forgiving the person with the
  disorder—and ourselves. Forgiveness and compassion
  will defuse the resentment.

To monitor our feelings means to identify them accurately;
then we need to express them appropriately. These are valuable

skills for everyone. But for the family and friends of a person with mental illness, they are essential for a balanced life.

When we are able to monitor and express our feelings properly, we eliminate a lot of confusion and anxiety. We know what is going on within us. We can name our feelings accurately so we can claim them honestly. This ability is a key aspect of self-care because proper monitoring keeps our emotional life in balance. It is one of the hallmarks of emotional maturity.

This skill especially comes into play in our relationship with our loved one with the disorder. The emotional life of a person with mental illness is by nature unstable. Emotional balance is one of the primary casualties of mental illness. If we are not emotionally stable and mature, we will become enmeshed in our loved one's emotional volatility. And because our loved one's well-being is so important to us, we are particularly upset by unhealthy, destructive, and stressful experiences when they do occur.

We can also take care of ourselves by minimizing the tension, confusion, and frustration in other parts of our lives. Sometimes, monitoring our feelings and expressing them to others in our network won't be enough. It's common for family and even friends to need professional help themselves—including counseling, medication, or both—if the stress and negative feelings turn into depression, anxiety, or other debilitating conditions. Hopefully, by learning about and accepting our loved one's disorder, we can address our own mental health needs in a timely way without guilt or feelings of failure. Self-care has a wide scope. Yes, we must attend to proper exercise, sleep, and diet. But we must also attend to our "outside" relationships that expand our focus beyond the illness, that refresh and satisfy us. We must monitor our own feelings and respond to others in the network. And we must take care of our own emotional and mental health. All of these areas help create our opportunity for a balanced life.

STORIES OF Hope
· · · · · · · · · ·

Self-Care Is Not Selfishness

For years, my husband's depression had been the center of our lives. He doesn't take his medication faithfully, so there are times when his symptoms are very bad. I took care of him to the point of becoming codependent. He was grateful most of the time, but after a while, I became worn out and resentful. I wanted to get away at times but felt guilty about it, so I never left him except to go to work. When he couldn't work anymore, he typically slept most of the day, and when I came home, I'd spend the evening and night mainly taking care of him.

This pattern went on for a few years, and he became even less responsible about taking his meds and seeing a counselor. We got into arguments about taking the medication, and I couldn't force him or convince him to do so. It's hard for me to say no. It's hard for me not to help someone who needs help, but my frustration increased, and I felt terrible for both of us.

A co-worker who knew my situation suggested that I attend a support group for people who have a loved one with mental health problems. I did, and through that group, I connected with a counselor. Both the counselor and the group members helped me see my situation more clearly. One of their messages to me was to take care of myself. They pointed out that looking after my legitimate needs is not selfish, but necessary for my own health, both physical and emotional. It took me some time, but I eventually saw the wisdom of that approach.

It was unfortunate and very difficult, but I saw no other alternative but to move into my own apartment.

I still love my husband and I hope we can get back together, but he must take the steps necessary to manage his illness.

Since I moved out of the house, I have experienced some peace and general well-being for the first time in years. I can tell that my emotional life is improving, and I am definitely a happier person. My husband continues to struggle along, and he has turned more to his parents and siblings for some of the things I did all those years. I truly wish him well, and I am willing to do what I can for him, but it is much clearer to me now what I can do and what I cannot do. My hope is that these new boundaries will eventually lead him to assume more responsibility for his mental health.

It's hard to tell where the line is between his own lapses in responsibility and the effects of the depression. I think that with him, that line changes depending on his current phase of depression. I do know that the way we were going was disastrous for me and not helpful for him. At this point, I am confident that I made the right decision.

Sorting Out My Feelings

My daughter was diagnosed with bipolar illness after she was married and had one child and was pregnant with her second. As I look back on her life, I can see some hints of the mania, although it never reached the point of being a real problem. But when she became very manic at this stage of her life, it was obvious that she needed some professional help. She agreed to see a psychiatrist, and after an initial adjustment period, she stabilized on her medication and saw a counselor regularly.

During this period, I lived nearby, so as her mother

and the grandmother of her children, I was part of her family as a babysitter and socially, too. I had often wondered if my divorce from her father had anything to do with her illness. I know that mental illness is not usually caused by an event like a divorce, but I also know that some difficult circumstances can trigger some long-standing emotional problems. I worried that my divorce might have played a part in her illness.

My daughter and son-in-law talked about possibly having more children, and when my daughter asked her psychiatrist about it, he took her off her medication, since some of the meds create a risk for a fetus. Within two months, my daughter was in the middle of a serious manic phase. I had moved out of state by this time, but I went back to help take care of the grandkids and ease my daughter back into a more stable emotional state.

By this time, I had sorted through my feelings about her illness and my role more clearly. I don't believe that my divorce had that great an impact on her illness. I knew that in the past, I would have taken over the care of the grandkids and the household. But I also knew that I probably would have resented that full-time responsibility. Taking care of myself while I also helped my daughter and her family was my goal.

I made arrangements with my son-in-law (who is very supportive of his wife) and another daughter who lives in the area to share the babysitting duties during the month that I was there. My bipolar daughter was free to visit her counselors, see her psychiatrist, and take care of herself while the rest of us worked together to meet the other responsibilities. My daughter eventually stabilized to the point where she could resume her role.

What helped me the most through this crisis was

that I had identified my feelings and had a clearer picture of what I could do and not do. As it turned out, things went more smoothly than I had imagined, both for me and for my daughter's family.

. . . .

QUESTIONS FOR GROUP DISCUSSION OR PERSONAL REFLECTION

1. Describe the ways in which you experience the strain of caring for your loved one—physically, emotionally, intellectually, socially, and spiritually.
2. List what you're doing now to practice healthy habits for exercise, sleep, and diet as part of your daily routine.
3. Describe the relationships you have that do not include or involve your loved one with the disorder. Do you need to expand these relationships?
4. How well do you balance your relationship with your loved one and your relationships with other family members and friends?
5. Are you aware of any resentment from other family members or friends because of the additional time and energy you give to the loved one with the disorder? If so, what can you do about this resentment?
6. This chapter outlines a four-step process to reduce resentment. How well do you think you can apply this process if resentment surfaces in your network of family and friends?
7. How well do you monitor your feelings? Are you seeking help to meet your own mental health needs?

CHAPTER SEVEN

.... Intentional Networks

STRATEGY *7* *Become a supportive network
of family and/or friends who know
about the mental disorder and
who commit to acting in the best
interest of our loved one as far as
we are able.*

W hat does the term "network" mean? When applied to people, it implies a system or an association of people who connect with one another at various points around a common interest or goal. For this strategy, a network can involve a wide variety of relationships, all revolving around one person: the person with mental health problems. The heart of this network will be the person's family and friends, whose common purpose is to provide emotional and social support for their loved one—and for themselves. Another tier in your network includes the professionals who meet the medical, psychological, and social needs of your loved one: the psychiatrist, nurse practitioner, social worker, therapist, occupational therapist or counselor, teachers, and so on. These are the paid members of your network whom you must identify, engage with, and maintain over time as you supplement their care with your network of family and friends.

Family and friends do not automatically become a supportive network just because they all have a relationship with the same loved one. A supportive network is intentionally made, and to become a part of it is a personal decision with practical consequences. To be effective, each person must commit to learning about the disorder and to helping the loved one and each other, each to his or her own ability. This is essential to forming a real network, as opposed to a group of people who merely happen to know the person.

Some family members and friends will decide that they do not want to be part of the network. It may be because they don't want to get involved too closely with someone with a mental disorder, even if that person is a good friend or a member of their family. This choice is more common with friends, but even some close relatives choose to distance themselves from their parent, child, or sibling because they don't want or can't handle the complications that accompany any close relationship with a person with mental illness.

In some cases this decision is understandable, especially for friends who have less time and emotional energy invested in the relationship. Most people have complicated lives, with many commitments and priorities, both personal and practical. A deeper commitment to a loved one with mental health problems requires time, dedication, and patience. Usually, no one knows this commitment better than the loved one's parents. Often, these parents are reluctant to ask for assistance because they are aware of the difficulties of providing this care and don't want to impose on people. They also may still be influenced by the stigma attached to mental illness and want to protect themselves and their loved one from possible ridicule or other negative reactions. As a result, these primary caregivers may assume complete responsibility of supporting their loved one. Before long, the strain takes a heavy toll, especially if the caregivers do not practice good self-care (see strategy 6).

The primary caregiver is not always a parent or two-parent team. It may be a sibling, spouse, or other family member—even a child taking care of a parent—or a friend, but the eventual result is the same: emotional drain. The worry, anxiety, fear, and tension that come with the constant, close contact with the loved one lead to a lack of healthy balance in the caregiver's own life. For the caregiver's sake and the sake of the loved one, help is needed. A network supplies that help.

Creating a Network

How do we create an intentional network? It will not be easy. The reluctance of most people to make a commitment like this will limit potential candidates for this role. The obvious possibilities include parents, spouses, grandparents, children, siblings, and close friends and other relatives. Once you outline the expectations for people in the network—discussed below—invite the most likely candidates in this inner circle to become part of the network.

Some of the people from this inner group will likely decline your invitation, and this is their prerogative. It is important that this refusal be accepted at face value and that there are no hard feelings surrounding this decision. Presumably, the person with the mental illness will need lifelong support, in varying degrees, so the network should be built assuming that it will be needed for the long haul. It's possible that some people will commit only with the option of pulling out or cutting back as circumstances change. Others might say they cannot commit to the network now but may be willing to do so later, in a few months or even years. Be flexible and leave the door open for different levels and terms of commitment.

Continue to invite people on a personal basis, face to face, until you have some who commit to playing a role. How many people? Depending on your circumstances, the number may range from three to ten or even more. Usually, the larger the network, the better. Different people can then provide different levels and kinds of support.

This strategy, like the other eight, is for the long term, and ideally the makeup of your network should reflect both the current and possible future needs of your loved one. But its members can also change over time. If your loved one is a child or adolescent, right now perhaps the network needs someone with age-appropriate skills and interests. When that young person becomes more adult, he or she will require different kinds of support. In other words, this network can change to meet new needs. One member may be a key player for a number of years and then, for personal reasons, or because of changing needs, he or she may assume a different role.

Because people and needs change, you will need to always be open to inviting new people in. As you identify new needs, consider who might be incorporated into the network to meet those needs, even on a temporary basis. Some of these people will be the paid professionals your loved one requires; others will be other relatives and friends who can serve a specific role and are willing to lend a hand for that purpose.

There may be another "tier" of people already involved with your loved one. They're not "intentional" network members, but they provide valuable help on an occasional basis. These might include neighbors, less involved relatives, or religious or volunteer organization members who will occasionally cook a meal, drive your loved one to the doctor, run errands, help with household repairs or chores, or babysit for an evening. Do welcome this assistance. And, if they seem open to it, invite these people to learn more about the mental illness and, gradually, assume more responsibilities within the network. Over time, they may be able to join with more intentionality.

When the primary caregiver is a mother or father, husband or wife, there is one specific fear that many of them express:

what will happen to our loved one when we die or are unable to care for him or her? Some parents and spouses agonize over this concern for decades. Establishing a stable and diverse network minimizes this concern. With a number of people involved, a plan for future care can emerge from discussions within the network. Such contingency plans might even be built into key network members' roles and responsibilities.

What Can a Network Do?

The responsibilities of a network vary according to the unique needs of the person with the disorder. Only the family and friends, with help from health care professionals, know the precise circumstances of the illness, the history and nature of relationships involved, and the personality of the loved one. The network itself, in conjunction with a counselor, if possible, determines the best way to support the loved one.

On the other hand, some general recommendations are helpful in determining the shared responsibilities within the network.

In-Home Companion Visiting

We all need caring companionship, and fresh perspectives can bring new interest and joy to our lives. The same goes for our loved one—perhaps even more so. Regular in-home visits from network members can broaden the person's social base and help build self-esteem and social skills. It is a "win-win" situation for everyone, including the companion, who learns more about the mental illness and has the chance to be a friend in a special, and often rewarding, relationship. This in-home companionship may be the single most valuable service a network can provide. Ideally, several people can share this role.

This service goes beyond the babysitting that is often provided by a teenager for young children. When mental illness is present, this role calls for an informed, mature adult, regardless of the age of the loved one. The more unpredictable the person's behavior, the more preparation and maturity is needed. Many primary caregivers are so worried about this volatility that they seldom, if ever, go out for their own recreation: they're not confident that anyone else could handle what might happen with the loved one. Even if they recognize the value of getting away regularly, they may feel they are not in a position to do that responsibly.

To solve this dilemma, a primary caregiver can ask some people in the network to prepare themselves to provide this service. These designated people might agree to attend a support group or educational program on mental illness. One option is to connect them with the Karla Smith Foundation (www.karla smithfoundation.org), the source of the strategies in this book. (And this book itself is a teaching tool and a good means of establishing consistency.) Other organizations, professionals, and guides offer similar approaches, but the result is that the network person will be better equipped as a companion. The primary caregivers can then feel comfortable taking a break that is long enough to provide a true respite. They can be confident that the care companion will be able to deal with most situations that may arise.

Outside-the-Home Activities

Network members can also lend a hand by doing errands, offering rides, and so on. They might go grocery shopping or take the loved one to school, to the park or a movie, to visit a friend, or to a health care appointment, for example. While these activities may not involve extended direct contact with the person, they can be very valuable to the person and to the caregivers, especially if done on a regular, scheduled basis. When these helpers are properly educated about the mental illness, they also lend emotional support both to the loved one and to the primary caregivers.

Each network differs in its makeup. As people commit to being members, they can determine and receive the proper training for the roles each of them will play.

Setting Realistic Expectations

It is important to spell out the expectations implied in accepting a network role. The intention is not to ask people to do things that they are incapable of doing or that are contrary to their personalities or interests. If someone is a sports fan, for example, he or she might include the person with mental illness in some sports-related activity. If someone has a hobby such as chess, wood-working, or knitting, perhaps they could include the loved one; if the loved one isn't familiar with that activity, it's an opportunity to learn a new skill. There are many possibilities, and until something has been tried, you shouldn't necessarily assume that your loved one wouldn't be interested, or couldn't handle it.

Regardless of the extent of involvement, the following expectations are reasonable and useful for network members:

- To be educated about the illness, to read books such as this one, and ideally to attend support group meetings or educational programs that explain the disorder and offer tips for family and friends (see chapter 3). As noted in strategy 3, anyone who relates to a person with mental illness in a significant way should have some knowledge of the symptoms, including possible unusual behaviors, so that they can respond appropriately to whatever might arise. This education also provides a valuable common understanding and language for all the people in the network.

- To know some details about the person's medication and the roles of the health care professionals, such as the doctor, counselor, or social worker. The helper should know the purpose, dosage, and possible side effects of all medications, where they are kept, where to get refills, and whom to contact in case of an emergency.

- To commit to the network for some time; the exact time frame can be open-ended, but, although not necessarily a lifelong commitment, this is more than just helping out once in a while. The idea is to create and maintain a relatively stable set of relationships that benefit both the loved one and the primary caregivers for a long enough period to ensure some continuity and consistency of care. It's possible that after being involved for some time, a person may decide to leave the network, and this decision should be accepted gracefully. The person might have ideas for where new members can be sought.

• To agree to meet periodically with the other network members, to compare observations, prepare for future needs, or adjust the roles within the network. This meeting could be held monthly, quarterly, or semiannually, depending on needs and circumstances. (It might be compared to the "staffing" meetings held in hospitals and treatment centers.) These periodic sessions are especially helpful if the loved one is a child or adolescent, because young people's needs can change significantly as they mature. The nature of the network evolves as the loved one becomes an adult, but the need for a network remains.

When inviting someone to become part of a network, be clear about these expectations and any others that are specific to the situation. Some aspects of the role and the relationship may not be easy to predict, so there may be surprises, which can be addressed as they occur. But the point is to be as clear and up-front about these expectations as possible—and to convey appreciation for the person's support.

Extended Networks

Beyond this immediate, personal network, there are local and national organizations that can help people with mental disorders and their family and friends. These include the National Alliance on Mental Illness (www.nami.org) and the Depression and Bipolar Support Alliance (www.dbsalliance.org) as well the Karla Smith Foundation already mentioned (www.karlasmithfoundation.org).

All are nonprofits dedicated to assisting people with mental health problems and their family and friends, and all offer various support groups. Joining a group of people experiencing similar life challenges can be a big step toward achieving a balanced life.

When a primary caregiver is unable to recruit a large enough network from among family and friends, it may be possible to recruit from the "unintentional" tier of people mentioned earlier: local religious congregations, charitable organizations, and clubs, for example. While these people may begin as occasional volunteers, perhaps even strangers, they can quickly become friends. Their willingness to help in the first place may indicate a familiarity with mental illness issues, and perhaps they already know the person at least a bit. Ideally, they will also be willing to increase their education about mental illness and even attend support group meetings and workshops. Over time, they may wish to become part of the more "intentional" network.

Let's end our discussion of this strategy with a caution and an admission. For all primary caregivers and network members, no matter how much knowledge and energy they bring to the task, there are limits on what they can do for the person with mental health problems. "Do what you can" is a wise slogan that will help everyone set reasonable expectations. There are two parts to the slogan: *Do,* meaning actually do it, and *what you can,* meaning accept your limitations. Most family members and friends are involved because they want to help their loved one erase the frustration, find some balance, enjoy some peace, and look to the future with hope. Sometimes they are dealing with a mental illness that is so baffling and frustrating that those dreams seem impossible. "Do what you can" reminds us to accept our limitations, get as much help as we can from our network, and leave the rest to our Higher Power (see strategy 9).

The purpose of this strategy, like all the other strategies, is to act in the best interest of our loved one and ourselves. To perceive that "best interest" takes knowledge and commitment. It also means that we all need help. Creating a network to share in the responsibilities of caregiving is a smart, effective way to broaden the knowledge, share the commitment, and get the help both the loved one and family and friends need.

STORIES OF Hope
....

Sharing the Struggle

I have a son who is schizo-affective and a mother who is obsessive-compulsive, so I have been around mental illness all of my life. At some point in my adulthood, it became clear that we would all be better off if we were open about the illnesses. It takes a lot of energy and, frankly, lies, to keep their behavior secret or invent excuses that make them seem more rational than they are. I didn't see the point in trying to keep up that kind of charade. It is hard enough dealing with the illnesses. I didn't need the added burden of trying to cover it up for other family members and friends.

I don't volunteer the truth to strangers, but I do mention their disorders when I talk about them with people who are truly interested. I found it to be a very freeing experience. The reactions of other people vary from shock to acceptance. The quick acceptance usually comes from people who also know someone with a mental illness. The shock reaction is due either to the mental health issues themselves or to the fact that I talk about them. I have learned that their reaction is not my problem, and that I have enough to cope with without being worried about what other people think.

It isn't like these mental health issues will be cured. They will not go away, and it took me a long time to come to that level of acceptance. Recovery is possible to the extent that my son and my mother will comply with all the medication, counseling, and sound advice they can get, but I don't think that in my case all of these circumstances will come together on a permanent basis. I believe I will spend the rest of my life being related to someone who has an untreated or ineffectively treated mental illness.

It helps, too, to belong to a support group for the families and friends of someone with a mental health problem. In that group, people can share their stories, struggles, hopes, and successes with other people who can identify with their feelings immediately. There is no need to go into long explanations about what it is like to love someone with a mental illness. I don't find that kind of acceptance and encouragement from people who don't have the experience. In the group, we can get to the issues quickly, and people's suggestions often provide practical help in concrete situations.

My willingness to talk about the mental health problems of my son and mother, and my participation in a support group, are two ways to create a network of support for me and my family. But I know that this strategy also calls for an expanded network of primary caregivers. This is the level I need to work on now. If I could find one or two more people to share the caregiving in practical ways, it would be much better for all of us. I have some people in mind, and soon I intend to ask them about it.

Who Will Help?

As parents of four children, one of whom is bipolar, we have our hands full. We love our children and feel blessed as a family. But we are the first to admit that our son's bipolar diagnosis creates some added stress in our family life. He's now nine years old. His behavior at times is almost unmanageable, and sometimes his treatment of his siblings means that we parents must step in and attend both to him and to them.

Preschool didn't turn out too well for him, so we homeschool the children. That is actually working out, and we plan to continue it on a year-by-year basis. We have a very good psychiatrist for him who monitors his medication closely and makes changes when it is necessary. There are periods of time when our son is less affected by his illness, and he is a very generous, bright, and loving child.

We joined a support group for the family and friends of people with mental health problems, and we find the sharing, information, and supportive relationships very helpful. It is one of the ways we try to create a network of people who can help us cope with our situation. Another couple in the group also has a child with mental health problems, and we try to meet up with them before the meeting for dinner and some socializing. Since many of our friends simply do not understand what we experience, it is refreshing to visit with another couple who are in a similar situation.

My mother babysits for us when we attend our meetings. She knows our circumstances and relates well with the children. But we can't ask her to care for the children too often, because it can be quite stressful. We can't get a regular babysitter because we don't know how our son will react, and we can't expect a teenager to handle what might happen.

We are making it at this point, but as the children get older, we know we will have to find more help. We are looking now for people and ways to expand our network. With two or three additional people who know our children and our situation, and who would be willing to help in practical ways, we would all experience a much better, more peaceful, and more nurturing family life.

. . . .

QUESTIONS FOR GROUP DISCUSSION
OR PERSONAL REFLECTION

1. How large, and how close, is your current support network for your loved one?

2. What are some options for when someone you invite into the network declines?

3. How extensive do you think your network should be? Do you have a plan for expanding your network as the need arises?

4. How well would the "in-home companion visits" and the "outside-the-home activities" benefit you? If you haven't planned for these yet but need to, what are the barriers and how can you overcome them?

5. What other services could your network provide that it isn't already providing?

6. Do you agree with the expectations outlined for becoming part of a network? Are there others that you would add for becoming part of your network because of your circumstances?

7. Do you find it difficult to "do what you can" and accept your limitations in helping your loved one? What can you do to practice this suggestion in the future?

CHAPTER EIGHT

Warning Signs

STRATEGY *8 Identify the early warning signs
that precede a more difficult phase
of the mental illness, and help our
loved one when these signs emerge.*

At times, the workings of the mind of a
person with mental health problems can be unpredictable. Their
motivations can seem inscrutable, their behavior unreliable, and
their emotions exaggerated and disjointed.

Of course, a person without a mental illness can also be unpredictable, inscrutable, and unreliable, with exaggerated and
disconnected emotions. But a person with such a disorder expresses these characteristics more frequently or more intensely,
and with less ability to recognize them as a problem or control
how and when they are expressed. Indeed, this is part of what
defines a mental disorder. Loving this person means being willing to accept this reality and trying to recognize and interpret
these characteristic behaviors and respond appropriately.

Family and friends are likely to be the first to notice any changes in the way the person thinks, feels, or acts, whether the clues are subtle or obvious. Being able to effectively interpret and respond to these changes is only possible if we know three things:

* the typical symptoms of the illness
* our loved one's typical reactions to medication
* our loved one's normal personality

All three of these factors are significant. We must have intimate knowledge of all three to detect the early warning signs that precede or begin a more difficult phase of the mental illness.

Recall strategy 1, on medication, and strategy 3, on education. If we've applied those strategies, we know about our loved one's medications and illness symptoms. Now recall strategy 5, on acceptance. Especially if we've practiced acceptance, we probably understand the unique personality of our loved one, with all its ups, downs, and other quirks. With informal, close, personal monitoring of our loved one, we can better distinguish whether a behavior is an expression of the symptoms of the illness, the effects or side effects of the medication, or the loved one's unique personality—or a combination of two or all three, as is often the case. The better we can discern these differences, the better we can identify the early warning signs of a more difficult phase.

Generally, the more severe the illness, the more intense and frequent the shifts in behavior—although even the most dramatic changes usually begin with subtle cues. There are some illnesses, however, such as borderline personality disorder, where the symptoms are more continuous than cyclic, and the fluctuations in behaviors may be less discernable. In these cases, the family and friends will have to modify this strategy as needed. Whatever the case, early preventive action can be extremely valuable, even in situations where it is difficult to detect changes in the intensity of the illness.

Warning Signs That Call for Intervention

As we know, each person with mental health problems expresses the illness in a unique way. Still, there are some common, predictable signs of a decline in mental health. Stay on the lookout for these signs:

- a shift from a regular sleep pattern to an irregular one
- a sudden or uncharacteristic increase in irritability
- an inability to relax after a period of relative calm
- conversations that show sudden or unusually disjointed or bizarre ideation
- more frequent or exaggerated fears
- sudden or more frequent expressions of misplaced or exaggerated anger
- unusual weight gain or loss
- becoming more isolated

Which of these apply to your loved one? What others can you think of that might be specific to your loved one? It's wise for caregivers to keep an ongoing list of these signs, based on their own observations and feedback from health care professionals, sponsors, and other members of the network. Share the list with the network. That way, everyone can stay on the lookout for these signs as an integral part of their caring relationship with their loved one.

When one or more members of the network notice any of these signs, they can consult with the other members, especially the primary caregivers, to determine if an intervention is needed.

The next step might be for the primary caregivers to call or visit the counselor, psychiatrist, or other health care professional, ideally with the loved one along. Here they can all discuss their observations and seek professional advice. It is best if the primary caregivers have already entered into an agreement with the health care professional to outline the conditions under which an intervention will take place. It is most helpful to establish this arrangement as the network is being formed. Preparation for all possibilities will ease the tension when something unusual begins to happen. Key members of the network should implement the plan as early as possible in order to avoid the most serious consequences of the declining behavior.

The intervention is a process, not just a specific, isolated action. It begins with the network members' observations and discussions and continues with the visit or call to the professionals by network representatives, preferably with the person with mental health problems included. The next steps can vary depending on the analysis of the first two steps. The intervention can lead to a change in medication, additional counseling sessions, adjusted living arrangements, or, if the decline is very debilitating or likely to result in harm to self or others, inpatient care at a behavioral health care facility. (Since inpatient care is limited by availability and cost, network members may become the extended "staff" of professional caregivers, at least temporarily.) After the intervention, the actions taken should be evaluated periodically and modifications made, if needed.

A central benefit of this network approach is that it raises the odds of early detection of any decline in the loved one's mental health. Early detection leads to early intervention.

Suicide Warning Signs

One of the deepest fears of many families and friends, expressed or unexpressed, is the possible suicide of their loved one. There are 30,000 suicides each year in the United States. That's a suicide every sixteen minutes. There is an attempted suicide every minute. Suicide is the third leading cause of death among fifteen-to twenty-four-year-olds.[8] And there are hundreds of thousands of people who are the family and friends of those who complete suicide, and more hundreds of thousands of family and friends of those who attempt it.

These statistics are alarming enough, but when you are close to someone with a mental illness, these numbers take on a personal and frightening face. Many, though not all, mental disorders increase the statistical likelihood of suicide. Even though they may not talk about it, the family and friends of people with mental illness usually are aware of this possibility and worry about it.

The American Association of Suicidology (AAS) has compiled a list of some possible warning signs that may lead to

Suicide Warning Signs

Get help immediately by contacting a mental health professional or calling the National Suicide Prevention Lifeline at 1-800-273-8255 for a referral should you witness, hear, or see anyone exhibiting one or more of these direct warning signs:

- threatening to hurt or kill him/herself, or talking of wanting to hurt or kill him/herself
- looking for ways to kill him/herself by seeking access to firearms, available pills, or other means
- talking or writing about death, dying, or suicide, when these actions are out of the ordinary for the person

These indirect warning signs may also warrant a call, as noted above. Does your loved one show any signs of these feelings or behaviors? Stay alert for them.

- hopelessness
- rage, uncontrolled anger, seeking revenge
- acting reckless or engaging in risky activities, seemingly without thinking
- feeling trapped, like there's no way out
- increased alcohol or drug use
- withdrawing from friends, family, and society
- anxiety, agitation, being unable to sleep, or sleeping all the time
- dramatic mood changes
- seeing no reason for living; no sense of purpose in life

suicide: signs that family and friends of a loved one with mental health problems are wise to be aware of. Those signs are summarized here as direct and indirect ones, followed by recommendations for helping a person who may be suicidal. All are adapted from the AAS Web site, www.suicidology.org.

Hopefully, the possibility of suicide is remote for your loved one. On the other hand, it is wise to be aware of the suicide warning signs and to talk about this possibility with a mental health professional when you establish your network.

Helping Someone Who Is Threatening Suicide

If a person is threatening suicide, or even hinting at it, pay close attention and keep this advice in mind:

- Be direct. Talk openly and matter-of-factly about suicide.
- Be willing to listen. Allow expression of feelings. Accept feelings.
- Be nonjudgmental. Don't debate whether suicide is right or wrong, or whether feelings are good or bad. Don't lecture on the value of life.
- Get involved. Become available. Show interest and support.
- Don't dare him or her to do it.
- Don't act shocked. This will put distance between you.
- Don't be sworn to secrecy. Seek support.
- Offer hope that alternatives are available but do not offer glib reassurances.
- Take action. Remove means, such as guns or stockpiled pills.
- Get help from persons or agencies specializing in crisis intervention and suicide prevention.

Stay alert so you can detect the warning signs of a decline in mental health. Then speak up and take positive action to understand and address those signs: this is one of the most loving acts you can do. This strategy complements the other strategies by giving you a specific preventive and practical plan for doing that.

STORIES OF Hope

Learning the Warning Signs

The major warning signs of our daughter's bipolar disorder were obvious. By the time she was into her deep depression, she could not get out of bed, could barely communicate, was extremely negative about herself and her worth, and would hardly eat. We couldn't miss the signs of her depression.

By the time she was fully manic, she was talking a mile a minute about unrelated topics, couldn't sleep, had grandiose plans about starting a university, felt the Mafia was after her, and was irritated that the rest of us didn't keep up with her or implement her plans. We couldn't miss the signs of her mania, either.

After both of these extreme experiences, we tried to pick up the less obvious signs of both her depression and her mania, so we could look for the cause of the change and take preventive action. At first, it wasn't easy to see the beginning signs of a significant change. Most of us have smaller versions of mood swings; some days we feel better than other days. Those ups and downs were normal for our daughter as well. We were faced with trying to distinguish these normal fluctuations from the beginning of a serious depressive or manic episode.

The key to identifying the true warning signs was ongoing awareness. We had to pay attention daily to her emotional state. Understandably, she got irritated if we asked her too often, "How are you feeling now?" But we became more observant. We simply watched and listened to her more intently, and then we tried not to jump to conclusions too quickly.

After a period of trial and error, the three of us in her immediate family got better at seeing when she was slipping into mania or depression. We shared our observations and together decided whether to confront her directly with what we observed.

This extra attention to her emotional state paid off a number of times. There was the time we noticed that she was gradually losing interest in a course at school that she previously liked, and she just seemed less enthusiastic in general. We mentioned it to her and encouraged her to talk to her counselor and then her psychiatrist. The result was a change in medication and an improvement in her attitude and feelings.

As time went on, we became much better at picking up on her emotional state and also at discussing it with her. Both of these had an added benefit: we had a better feel for the effects of her bipolar disorder and could identify with her experience more completely.

Differing Interpretations of Warning Signs

At this point, we still don't know whether our twenty-one-year-old daughter's situation is the beginning of a mental disorder or is an illegal-drug-induced reaction. In either case, her behavior, including a period when she refused to eat, is clearly abnormal and dangerous. Most of the time, she is uncooperative and seems to be in some stage of denial.

My other daughter, my husband, and I are all responding differently to her. It's hard to characterize how each of us is reacting because this whole experience is still relatively new. What I do know is that the combination of my daughter's condition and our conflicting reactions to it is very stressful.

To help me understand and cope with her and the changes in our family, I joined a support group and go to a counselor. Our situation is clearly not settled, and the confusion and anger remain, but I am beginning to see some hope for a little peace for me. My husband and other daughter didn't think it was necessary to get help outside the family. They basically figured that we could handle things and that, in time, our troubled daughter would get better. I am convinced that this approach is wishful thinking and that things will not automatically improve.

I believe there are warning signs in our daughter's behavior that indicate truly serious issues. Since my husband doesn't see it the same way, it is causing some added tension in our relationship. When I asked him to go to a marriage counselor with me, he initially refused. My hope is now growing, however, because he changed his mind and agreed to go with me to the counselor. We have just begun the process, but I feel we are heading in the right direction.

I have also found that, regardless of how my husband and two daughters deal with this confusing situation, I need some time alone at home to keep my balance. When I feel it is necessary, I retreat to our bedroom and spend some quiet time thinking and relaxing. I have come to value these private times because I could not deal with the constant anxiety that all too often is now part of our family life.

The warning signs are clear. But without a good diagnosis, we are dealing with symptoms and signs and not the basic cause of her problems. I am confident that the doctor will eventually be able to name the problem. The anticipation of that diagnosis gives me hope. We don't know how things will turn out with our daughter or with our family, but the counseling and my personal time are two steps that will help me find some peace in the midst of this confusion and struggle.

. . . .

QUESTIONS FOR GROUP DISCUSSION OR PERSONAL REFLECTION

1. Which of your loved one's possible behaviors do you fear the most?
2. Within your own circle of family or friends, did anyone end or significantly alter their relationship with you, your loved one, or both because of the mental illness? What were the circumstances of this change in the relationship?
3. To what extent does your loved one's mental illness change periodically? Describe these changes.
4. What early warning signs of possible future difficulties have you noticed in your loved one?
5. How would an intervention take place in your situation?
6. Have you been fearful of the possible suicide of your loved one? If so, how have you handled this fear? What practical steps have you taken to try to prevent or intervene on this possibility?

CHAPTER NINE

...............Faith

STRATEGY *9 Acknowledge our dependence*
on a Higher Power and seek
guidance from that Higher
Power in whatever way that is
comfortable to us.

Recent polls have shown that the vast ma-
jority of people in the United States believe in the existence of
a Higher Power, which most call God.[9] The specific name for
God varies by religious affiliation. The three major monotheistic
religions in the world—Christianity, Judaism, and Islam—as
well as Hinduism, all hold to the existence of a Supreme Being,
though they all describe and name this Being differently. While
Buddhists don't believe in a deity per se, they do revere and follow the Buddha as the model for transcending suffering and
achieving enlightenment.

The use of the term "Higher Power" here is intended to neutralize the differences among people of varying beliefs. This use

is consistent with the efforts of Twelve Step and other programs to unite people around the need for a spiritual practice or belief system without insisting on specific formulations of what that belief system is.

The recommendations in this strategy, then, are spiritual in nature, rather than religious. What do we mean by "spiritual"? Here, we're referring to the sense that there is more to life than meets the eye—a dimension of reality that goes beyond scientific analysis, verifiable historical data, or even psychological insights. For many of us, it's that sense of mystery when we face life's big questions. For most people, the answers to this mystery are satisfied by their belief in God. For people who do not have an active faith in God, their Higher Power may be the combined wisdom, knowledge, and care expressed by a group of people—perhaps even a support group. Or it might be a special connection with nature.

For those of us close to a person with a mental illness, the other eight strategies discussed in this book can be strengthened by incorporating this dimension of faith or belief, however we express it.

In discussions with other members of the network, we refrain from trying to convert them to our religious convictions or spiritual beliefs. We may state our beliefs honestly, but also with respectful acceptance of other people's beliefs and in the spirit of finding common ground in our need for mutual support.

To acknowledge our reliance on a Higher Power implies that we are not in complete control of our own lives—or anyone else's. The need for this reliance becomes obvious as we try to cope with the mental illness of a loved one. It may take time for us to admit that we're not in complete control and need to rely on a Power greater than ourselves. When we first face our loved one's baffling behavior and illogical thought patterns, we believe we can find a way to control and correct this behavior. This is especially true when our loved one is young. When all our efforts prove fruitless, or only minimally beneficial, we become more frustrated. Gradually, usually through the painful process of getting a diagnosis and learning more about the illness, we do face our powerlessness. We do what we can, but, in the final analysis, we must acknowledge that we cannot "fix" the illness by ourselves—or even with all the professional help and support we can muster.

The strategies in this book all outline effective ways to cope with mental illness and find hope for a balanced life. A key component of this balance, however, is the realization that although we cannot control the illness completely, we can find strength and hope in turning over to our Higher Power the things we can't control or "fix." This reliance is not an escape from the reality of the mental illness. We are simply accepting the limits of our understanding and our ability to help. We are accepting our need to look outside ourselves for this strength and hope.

Working these nine strategies may lead some people to change their concept of a Higher Power. Face to face with the challenges of coping with mental illness, they may find themselves questioning their belief in a Higher Power—perhaps especially if their concept was based on a childhood notion of a God that they hadn't questioned until now. Normally a child's idea of God does not incorporate complexities and contradictions such as those that arise when we confront mental illness. For people facing this challenge, it's important to do some soul-searching. Perhaps it will lead to a more flexible, mature understanding of a Higher Power, one that they can turn to for support—one that gives them hope even as they face the reality of their loved one's mental illness.

Seeking Guidance

How do we seek the guidance of a Higher Power in supporting our loved one? In religious communities, we can seek it through prayer, consultation with spiritual leaders, support groups, personal meditation, reading, and worship. People unaffiliated with a religious community can seek this guidance through reading, reflection, support groups, and consultation with people they trust to offer wisdom and support.

To seek guidance implies that we express our fears, concerns, and difficulties to our Higher Power. Whether we express them openly or within our own minds and hearts, we admit that we are troubled and need help. While we can also express our gratitude for successes, such as finding a medication that works, we especially need to seek guidance for coping with those aspects of the mental illness that confuse and frustrate us. We admit that we want and need help.

But we do not know whether or how that guidance might emerge. When we seek, therefore, it is best to do so without expectations. We simply present our situation to our Higher Power. It can be very easy to confuse setting expectations with seeking guidance, because it's natural to anticipate a desired outcome. We want this illness to go away, and when we discover that we can't banish it ourselves, we want our Higher Power to take it away miraculously. But with time, we find that we are seeking guidance for coping with the continuing reality of the illness, not for making it disappear.

For each of us, the way our Higher Power answers our plea resides in our own heart and mind. Often we frame those answers within our own faith or belief system. Some people may testify that while they are in the act of seeking guidance from their Higher Power, they will experience an "answer" or a sense of direction or a sense of peace that eases some of the anxiety. For others, guidance comes slowly, some time after the act of seeking it. It can assume the form of a gradual understanding or acceptance of a particular course of action. In these cases, the guidance often comes from within, after reflection and time.

Sometimes, the guidance may show itself through circumstances that change for the good, perhaps unexpectedly. For example, a loved one is suddenly extricated from a seemingly intractable, troubling relationship. Or a family gathering winds up being enjoyable for everyone—an event a family member had been dreading because it's typically stressful for her and her loved one. At the time, you might not have linked these better-than-anticipated outcomes with the guidance you'd sought from your Higher Power, but in retrospect, you're able to make those connections.

You may also connect the advice and action of your loved one's psychiatrist, counselor, coach, or support group with finding guidance from your Higher Power.

Prayer

One of the most common ways of seeking guidance from a Higher Power is prayer. There are, of course, many forms of prayer, and most religious traditions and spiritual paths have particular, preferred prayers and rituals. If prayer is the way you seek guidance, then pray in whatever way is comfortable to you.

The Serenity Prayer has proven universally helpful for people in Twelve Step groups, where reliance on a Higher Power is also encouraged. The four-line prayer was written by Reinhold Niebuhr. I have added a second verse that was composed by our daughter Karla Smith before she died. As the official prayer of the Karla Smith Foundation, it is an appropriate ending to this section of the book.

> God, grant me the serenity
> To accept the things I cannot change,
> Courage to change the things I can,
> And wisdom to know the difference.
>
> Show me the trace of you in everyone I know.
> Gently turn my gaze back home, toward simplicity, grace,
>   and gratitude.
> Remind me that we are all imperfect, holy, and free.
> Open me to know and embrace your peace.

STORIES OF .... Hope

Dependence on God

Living with an adult son who has struggled with drugs and depression for about thirty years, I have learned the hard way that I am powerless over his depression, his drugs, and him. My fears were—and still are—that he will self-medicate with drugs to treat his anxieties and deep depression. His cycle of recovery and then relapse has been a circle with no end in sight, but I have found some hope and peace through the support of others and a counselor for our son.

In this situation and others, I have turned to God. Reminding myself that I am powerless is perhaps as important as reminding myself that our son is power-less. My faith in God has been a source of comfort throughout my life, but I don't expect God to do my will. I pray that God will take away my son's depression and addiction, but I know that God doesn't always do what I want.

I am convinced that God is a loving God and that we have frailties and limitations that sometimes baffle us. Life can be hard, but God understands and accepts us with our limitations. Turning to God for comfort and guidance helps me keep a more positive perspective on our son's illness and addiction.

Only our son, with God's help, can achieve recovery. My role is to be there for him in whatever way I can. We have experienced relapse so often, with multiple treatment centers, AA sponsors, doctors, counselors, and medications that I sometimes feel like there is noth-ing left to try. My prayer then is more for acceptance, with less focus on recovery. Sometimes I feel that God comforts me by being with me in my frustration and disappointment, even though the problems do not go away.

On the other hand, there are some wonderful moments when our son is clean and balanced. During those times, his kindness and thoughtfulness come forward, and I see him for the truly loving person he is. These times *are* answers to my prayers. Even when these interludes of sobriety, peace, and balanced emotional life last for only a few weeks, it does give us a chance to relate to our "real son," unencumbered by the drugs and depression. I am truly grateful for these periods. At one time, my prayers were for a complete cure—a miracle of transformation—but I have come to appreciate the periodic clean, balanced times as gifts from God and from our son.

I have learned to be thankful for less. Realistically, even though I still long for a complete and permanent recovery, I may never see more than temporary periods of relative balance. But I thank God for that much, and I know that God is also with me in the troubled times.

"There Was Nothing I Could Do"

On the day after my daughter's second suicide attempt, I made a desperate call to the last doctor who had evaluated her. I knew he had successfully treated cases like hers, and I had been so pleased when my daughter agreed to an appointment with him. Unfortunately, after one session, she refused to return. She really didn't think she had a problem after all.

The half-day in the hospital emergency room, with the uncomfortable procedures and the probing questions, had gotten her attention. I was hoping she would now agree to see the doctor regularly, and I also hoped

that he would have some words of wisdom for a trau-
matized mom caught in a battle that was feeling increasingly overwhelming.

Upon hearing about the suicide attempt, the recep-
tionist put me through quickly to the doctor. He asked
to speak to her directly, and after a bit of discussion,
my daughter handed the phone back to me. Since she
was refusing to meet with him for medicine and therapy, there was nothing he could do for her.

I then asked him how I could help her. What could
I say? What could I do? She had not been receptive at
all to my previous attempts to guide her to help. He
replied, very kindly but rather bluntly, that there was
nothing I could do. People with this disorder, he said,
frequently attempt suicide, not because they want to
die, but because they want to lash out at someone else
and make them feel guilty. Unfortunately, a significant
percentage of these people do die as a result of one of
these attempts. And until she decided to get help, there
was nothing at all I could do.

"You mean I can only sit here and watch her ruin
her life?" I asked incredulously. "I'm afraid so," he
replied.

Any hope left inside me at that point was instantly
dashed as I came face to face with the fact that there
was nothing I could do to fix my daughter's problems.
Her future, at age seventeen, was an increasingly tenta-
tive series of "ifs": She had a chance *if* she would accept
the fact that she needed help, and *if* she would agree
to reach out for it, and *if* we could find a good doctor,
and *if* she liked him or her enough to keep going, and
if the doctor found medication that would help, and *if*
she was able to pull her life back together enough to
continue her education, and *if* she could handle college
despite her emotional struggles, and *if* all of this happened before she suffered the consequences of a bad de-

cision that could prematurely end her life, or negatively impact the rest of it. The whole life that lay before my sweet, pretty, smart daughter was being held hostage by a brutal mental illness that she had to fight, at least initially, entirely alone.

Several weeks later, our scripture study group at church was studying a particular Bible story. It told of a paralyzed man whose friends removed a section of roof above the place where Jesus sat, and lowered the man down to Jesus to be healed. The words leapt out of the book at me: "When Jesus saw their faith, He said to the paralytic, 'Child, your sins are forgiven.'" What stunned me were the words "*their* faith." The paralytic may or may not have had faith of his own, but his friends' faith was sufficient for the healing. There was something I could do after all—I could pray and exercise my faith on my daughter's behalf.

Getting my daughter to recognize that she had to reach out for help was impossible for me. But nothing is impossible for God.

Soon, a woman came to my daughter's high school to speak to an all-student assembly about her experience with the illness of depression. She, too, had attempted suicide. But she eventually reached out and had been prescribed a medication that corrected her brain chemistry. She was once again able to enjoy life. She urged anyone experiencing these same feelings to get help.

It was the afternoon after that assembly that my daughter asked me to get her an appointment with a doctor. This time, she stuck with the medication and the appointments, and, thankfully, her future continues to look much brighter.

"It Seemed Easy Enough"

My son's kindergarten teacher had told her students to look out a window of their house and draw what they saw. It seemed easy enough: a simple homework assignment. No one was expecting the realism or the symbolic interpretation of a great master of the Renaissance—just a child's rendering of a view from a window.

Nevertheless, the assignment drove my ADHD son into a complete and total meltdown that afternoon. After just a few moments of sketching the window frame and the outlines of a couple of trees, he was viciously stabbing his paper with the pencil. Then he was crumpling and tearing and throwing the paper, and everything else nearby, all the while crying and insisting that he was clearly stupid because he was incapable of accomplishing this much-too-difficult feat.

I couldn't remember reading anything in Dr. Spock's book about this. And I couldn't understand exactly what my son perceived to be the problem. Was he frustrated that his sketch didn't look realistic enough? Did he have no idea how to translate what he saw with his eyes onto a two-dimensional piece of paper? Did he really, really hate art enough that he didn't want to spend a few minutes drawing the trees in our yard? (This was a distinct possibility. He was the only child in his preschool class who routinely refused to do art projects—but all by himself he had figured out some very advanced math concepts.) Did the other kinds of homework he completed seem so easy to him that he was completely frustrated by the relative difficulty of this assignment?

My son's explanation for his distress was simply that it was "too hard." Nothing I said was alleviating his distress or making him more reasonable. I prayed for the wisdom to handle this situation effectively, having absolutely no clue how that would be, but knowing that God had all the answers.

It was then that I noticed the raccoon climbing slowly up one of the trees in the yard. My son loved animals, and this proved to be the perfect distraction. (For once, that short attention span was a blessing!) Both of us focused on the raccoon's journey to the top of the tree, where he eventually became hidden in the foliage. But he created an enjoyable distraction for long enough that my son calmed down and could once again hear what I was saying.

We took a break from homework for a couple of hours and spent some time talking about the assignment before he returned to it. He was eventually able, with significantly less frustration, to complete his drawing. I felt so grateful that he was able to turn in his assignment, rather than being embarrassed by not completing a task everyone else in the classroom probably considered very easy. And I felt blessed to have been given the insight that my son would always need some extra help focusing on and completing any right-brained (creative) tasks that were assigned as homework—an insight that remains helpful to both of us through even his high school years.

· · · · · · · · · · ·

QUESTIONS FOR GROUP DISCUSSION OR PERSONAL REFLECTION

1. For you, what does it mean to be spiritual?
2. Describe your Higher Power.
3. How does your personal faith or sense of spirituality apply to your relationship with your loved one?

4. Has your experience with mental illness changed your image of your Higher Power? If so, describe that change.

5. Is your Higher Power one that you can turn to for guidance?

6. If so, how do you seek guidance from your Higher Power?

7. What expectations do you have when you seek guidance from your Higher Power?

8. How have you found guidance from your Higher Power regarding your loved one's mental health problems?

9. Is the Serenity Prayer with the added stanza by Karla Smith meaningful for you? How?

............*Types of Mental Disorders*

Mental disorders, also referred to as mental illnesses or psychiatric disorders, affect almost one-fourth of adults in the United States at some time in their lives. Some people experience a disorder only once, as a single episode. Once their symptoms remit—ease up—they are gone for good. Other people experience several separate episodes, a condition referred to as recurrent mental illness. Months or years may pass between episodes, and the person functions well when the symptoms are in remission. Still others experience chronic or persistent mental illness in which some symptoms are always present. People with chronic symptoms are more likely to be disabled as a result. They must learn to manage their disorder for the long term, often for the rest of their lives. And some people have multiple disorders, too.

Let's look at some of the most common mental disorders. For some people, these may occur jointly.

....

The material contained in this appendix has been adapted from *A Family Guide to Coping with Dual Disorders: Addiction and Psychiatric Illness* by Dennis C. Daley and Janet Spear, Center City, MN: Hazelden, 2003.

Depressive Disorders

Depressive disorders, also referred to as mood or affective disorders, involve a mood disturbance or prolonged depressed emotional state. Depression affects up to 10 percent of men and 25 percent of women. (Of these, more than one-fourth also have an addictive disorder.) Symptoms can include depressed mood, loss of interest in usual activities or pastimes, poor appetite, sleep disturbance, fatigue, loss of energy, or suicidal tendencies. Some general types are major depression, dysthymia (a low-grade but chronic condition), and depression caused by a medical or addictive disorder. Major depression may be experienced as a single episode or as a recurrent disorder with multiple episodes over time. It may also include psychotic symptoms such as delusions.

Bipolar Disorder

Bipolar disorder, also referred to as manic depression, affects about 1 percent of the adult population and is a chronic, lifelong condition. About 60 percent of people with bipolar disorder also have an addictive disorder. As the name suggests, this illness involves wide mood swings between two poles: mania and depression. At one extreme is mania or hypomania—elevated, expansive, or irritable moods along with other symptoms, such as heightened activity, restlessness, or rapid, "pressured" speech. At the other extreme, the person's mood may switch to clinical depression. The person may have episodes at both extremes, or mixed episodes in which both manic and depressive symptoms are present at the same time. In more extreme forms, bipolar illness can include psychotic symptoms, cause severe problems, and be life threatening—up to 15 percent may die by suicide. In milder forms of the disorder, such as hypomania, the person may feel energized and productive during hypomanic episodes.

Anxiety Disorders

Under this category are a variety of disorders, each with a unique set of symptoms: phobias, panic disorder, generalized anxiety disorder, obsessive-compulsive disorder, and post-traumatic stress disorder. Addiction is common with anxiety disorders, especially dependence on prescription drugs such as tranquilizers.

Phobias involve persistent and irrational fears and avoidance of objects, activities, or situations. There are three major types. *Agoraphobia* involves a fear of being in public places or situations from which escape would be difficult. It may be accompanied by panic attacks: sudden and intense periods of fear, with physical symptoms such as heart palpitations, dizziness, sweating, trembling, shortness of breath, a feeling of choking or nausea, chills, or hot flashes. Fear of losing control or dying is common during a panic attack too. A *social phobia* involves a persistent and irrational fear of, and a desire to avoid, a situation where the person anticipates being scrutinized by others, for example, while speaking or eating in front of others. The person with this phobia is afraid that he or she may act in a way that is humiliating or embarrassing. A *specific phobia* is a persistent and irrational fear that is excessive or unreasonable. It often leads to avoiding certain things, such as animals, or situations, such as being in an enclosed space or flying in an airplane.

Panic disorder includes the unexpected panic attacks described above, followed by a concern that more attacks will occur. Panic disorder may also involve worry about the consequences of a panic attack, such as having a heart attack or losing control.

Generalized anxiety disorder (GAD) involves excessive feelings of anxiety and worry that are hard to control. They may be accompanied by shakiness, trembling, trouble relaxing, pounding heart, dizziness, upset stomach, fear that something bad will happen, and feeling on edge.

Obsessive-compulsive disorder (OCD) involves recurrent or intrusive thoughts (obsessions) and repetitive actions (compulsions) that are distressing and interfere with one's ability to function.

Obsessions include images or ideas that are unpleasant, such as thoughts of contamination, illness, violence, or making mistakes; they may also include a strong need for exactness and order. Compulsions are repetitive actions, often done in an attempt to counteract obsessions. They include repeating behaviors such as very frequent hand washing, checking doors or windows, counting or ordering, or tapping.

Post-traumatic stress disorder (PTSD) involves reexperiencing a traumatic event (such as rape, assault, combat, accident, or natural disaster) through recurrent dreams or recollections of the event. Those with PTSD may also experience a numbing of their responsiveness and a reduced involvement with the world.

Schizophrenia

Schizophrenia affects about 1 percent of the population, and almost half also have an addictive disorder. Schizophrenia is a brain disease with both positive and negative symptoms. With positive symptoms, something is present that should not be, such as hallucinations (hearing, seeing, feeling, or tasting things that do not exist in reality), delusions (false beliefs), illogical thinking or loose associations (ideas and thoughts that do not connect), inappropriate emotional responses, agitation, or bizarre behavior. With negative symptoms, something is missing or some kind of functioning is lost. Examples include withdrawal from people, inability to feel pleasure (anhedonia), trouble getting motivated to start or finish tasks, difficulty focusing attention, and "flat" emotions—that is, normal emotional responses are missing. These positive and negative symptoms all undermine the person's ability to function. Schizophrenia is one of the most chronic and debilitating mental illnesses.

Eating Disorders

These disorders, which include anorexia and bulimia, involve extreme disturbances in eating behaviors. A person with anorexia is intensely fearful of becoming obese. Typically, people with the disease also have a distorted body image, lose weight to an unhealthy extent, and refuse to maintain a normal body weight. Bulimia involves recurrent episodes of binge eating followed by a depressed mood and self-deprecating thoughts about the binges. People with bulimia may use self-induced vomiting, restrictive diets, and diuretics to purge what was eaten during the binges.

Personality Disorders

Personality disorders involve a long-term pattern of behavior that deviates from what is normal in the person's culture, appears in a variety of situations, and causes significant distress or impairment. A person with a personality disorder has a distorted view of him- or herself, others, and the world; problems controlling emotions and impulses; and/or relationship problems.

Borderline Personality Disorder (BPD)

BPD is much more common among women than men and affects about 2 percent of the total population; about two-thirds of those with BPD have an addiction. Many also have mood, anxiety, or eating disorders. People with this disorder typically have problems such as unstable and intense relationships; impulsiveness; rapid shifts of emotion; intense anger or problems controlling anger; suicidal threats, gestures, or behaviors; self-mutilation (cutting or burning one's own body); identity disturbance; chronic emptiness; and frantic efforts to avoid abandonment. Some with BPD experience psychotic symptoms.

Antisocial Personality Disorder (ASP)

ASP is much more common among men than women and affects a little over 2 percent of the total population. About 84 percent of those with ASP also have an addiction. This disorder involves a pattern of antisocial behavior in which the rights of others are violated. The person often breaks the law, deceives others, lacks guilt or remorse for behaviors, and is irresponsible and impulsive. People with ASP often begin abusing drugs and alcohol at an early age. They are often unemployed or under-employed due to poor school achievement, poor work history, and irresponsible behavior. Men with ASP are more likely than others to commit violent acts; many end up in jail or prison due to criminal behaviors.

APPENDIX B
............*Substance Use Disorders*

Addiction is diagnosed by a health care clinician trained in addiction medicine. The clinician interviews the person to gather details about alcohol and drug use, health, family, and personal history. Family members may also be interviewed, as some people with addiction minimize their substance use, and family members can provide more accurate information.

What Are the Symptoms of Addiction?

Addiction is characterized by obsession (the person thinks too much and too often about substances) and compulsion (the person uses repeatedly and cannot stop; in fact, the person "can't not use" and "needs" substances). Addiction is considered a disease by the American Medical Association. While there are

....

The material contained in this appendix has been adapted from *A Family Guide to Coping with Dual Disorders: Addiction and Psychiatric Illness* by Dennis C. Daley and Janet Spear, Center City, MN: Hazelden, 2003.

physical symptoms, most symptoms are psychological or behavioral. For many, addiction is also a "lifestyle" problem.

According to the American Psychiatric Association's *DSM-IV,* the person who shows three or more of the following symptoms within a twelve-month period is diagnosed with substance dependence or addiction.

1. Alcohol or drugs are taken in larger amounts or over a longer period than the person intended.
2. There is a persistent desire or one or more unsuccessful attempts to cut down or control substance use.
3. A great deal of time is spent in activities necessary to get the substance, take the substance, or recover from its effects.
4. Substance use interferes with major role obligations at work, school, and home, or the person uses when it is physically hazardous.
5. Important social, occupational, or recreational activities are stopped or reduced because of substance use.
6. The person continues to use substances, despite knowledge of having a persistent or recurrent social, psychological, or physical problem caused or worsened by such use.
7. The person develops tolerance—that is, a need for significantly increased amounts of the substance in order to achieve intoxication—or a markedly diminished effect with continued use of the same amount.
8. The person experiences withdrawal symptoms when substance use is stopped or reduced.
9. A substance is often taken to relieve or avoid withdrawal symptoms (drinking in the morning to relieve the morning "shakes," or using drugs continuously during the day to prevent withdrawal, for example).

However, your loved one may have a problem with alcohol or other drugs even if he or she does not meet these criteria for substance dependence. If substance use causes problems, "abuse" may be diagnosed. Although less severe than dependence, substance abuse still is a serious problem, particularly for people with mental disorders, because it impairs judgment; causes medical, psychological, and social problems; and interferes with treatment for a mental disorder. For example, alcohol abuse can lower the effectiveness of some psychiatric medications. Or drug use can lead to lower motivation to change and poor adherence to treatment plans.

Do not be surprised if your loved one denies or minimizes the problem. "Denial," a psychological defense, protects one from admitting the truth: in this case, having an addiction. People often believe that in order to be addicted, they have to use drugs or alcohol every day, lose control, get high or drunk every time they use, use "hard" drugs such as heroin, or suffer physical withdrawal. This simply is not true, as addiction can also exist in the absence of these symptoms, as long as other symptoms are present.

What Causes Addiction?

Many factors contribute to addiction. Psychological factors include personality, coping abilities, and beliefs about oneself and the world. Some people take more risks than others, and substance use is one form of risky behavior. Others depend on substances to cope with stress or emotional distress such as anxiety, depression, or boredom. Social factors contributing to substance use and addiction include pressures to use from family, friends, or people in the community.

Like many disorders, addiction has a genetic basis that runs in families. Studies show a significant increase in the risk of addiction for children in families in which a parent is addicted.

Alcohol and other addictive drugs such as cocaine and heroin work on the same area of the brain that is involved in making food and sex pleasurable. This part of the brain is called the "reward pathway" (or mesolimbic dopamine pathway). As the neurological basis for addiction has become known, substance dependence, like mental illness, is being called a brain disease.

Treatment for Addiction

Addiction is treated with counseling or therapy, rehabilitation or self-help programs, medications, or some combination of these. Treatment is more effective than many people may realize. Addiction is a chronic disease for most people, which means that problems and symptoms may return from time to time. While the ideal outcome is for your loved one to become and to stay sober, many people with an addiction relapse once or more. However, most show positive effects from treatment, and many who relapse eventually do stay sober. The most effective treatment approach for people with both mental illness and substance dependence is an integrated co-occurring disorders program, either inpatient or outpatient.

Therapy and rehabilitation programs help the addicted person learn "recovery skills," such as coping with cravings to use alcohol or other drugs, resisting pressures from others to use, handling upsetting situations or emotions without using, and seeking help and support from family members, friends, and others in recovery. Treatment encourages the person to become involved in Alcoholics Anonymous (AA), Narcotics Anonymous (NA), Cocaine Anonymous (CA), Dual Recovery Anonymous (DRA), or other mutual-support programs.

Professional treatment sometimes involves the family as well. Family members may be asked to attend sessions to learn more about addiction and to learn what they can and cannot do to help their loved one. If your loved one is receiving professional treatment, ask to attend some sessions and inquire about family education programs.

If your loved one refuses treatment, talk with an addiction

counselor about strategies to "pressure" him or her to enter treatment. This often works. However, there are some instances in which nothing that a family member does leads the addicted member to enter treatment. If you have tried everything and your loved one continues to refuse help, focus on detaching and taking care of yourself. Do not let this person drag you down emotionally. One good resource is Al-Anon, a Twelve Step program for family members of alcoholics and addicts, that can support you whether your loved one decides to get help or not.

The Twelve Steps
.............of Alcoholics Anonymous*

1. We admitted we were powerless over alcohol—that our lives had become unmanageable.
2. Came to believe that a Power greater than ourselves could restore us to sanity.
3. Made a decision to turn our will and our lives over to the care of God *as we understood Him.*
4. Made a searching and fearless moral inventory of ourselves.
5. Admitted to God, to ourselves, and to another human being the exact nature of our wrongs.
6. Were entirely ready to have God remove all these defects of character.
7. Humbly asked Him to remove our shortcomings.
8. Made a list of all persons we had harmed, and became willing to make amends to them all.

....

* From *Alcoholics Anonymous,* 4th ed., published by AA World Services, Inc., New York, N.Y., 59–60.

9. Made direct amends to such people wherever possible, except when to do so would injure them or others.

10. Continued to take personal inventory and when we were wrong promptly admitted it.

11. Sought through prayer and meditation to improve our conscious contact with God *as we understood Him,* praying only for knowledge of His will for us and the power to carry that out.

12. Having had a spiritual awakening as the result of these steps, we tried to carry this message to alcoholics, and to practice these principles in all our affairs.

..........Notes

1. Tom Smith with Kevin and Karla Smith, *The Tattered Tapestry: A Family's Search for Peace with Bipolar Disorder* (Lincoln, NE: iUniverse, 2005). The book is available through www.amazon.com and www.barnesandnoble.com.

2. President's Commission on Mental Health, *Achieving the Promise: Transforming Mental Health Care in America*, 2003. Find it online at www.mentalhealthcommission.gov/reports/FinalReport/toc.html.

3. Etienne Krug, Linda Dahlberg, James Mercy, Anthony Zwi, and Rafael Lozano, eds. *World Report on Violence and Health* (Geneva: World Health Organization, 2002).

4. Robert Bolton, *People Skills* (New York: Simon & Schuster, 1979).

5. Thomas Gordon, *Parent Effectiveness Training* (New York: Random House, 2000).

6. President's Commission on Mental Health, *Achieving the Promise: Transforming Mental Health Care in America*, 2003. Find it online at www.mentalhealthcommission.gov/reports/FinalReport/toc.html.

7. President's Commission on Mental Health, *Achieving the Promise: Transforming Mental Health Care in America*, 2003, p. 4. Find it online at www.mentalhealthcommission.gov/reports/ FinalReport/toc.html.

8. National Institute of Mental Health, *Suicide in the U.S.: Statistics and Prevention* (find it online at www.nimh.nih.gov/ health/publications/suicide-in-the-us-statistics-and-prevention .shtml). American Foundation for Suicide Prevention, *Facts and Figures, National Statistics* (find it online at www.afsp.org/index .cfm?fuseaction=home.viewPage&page_id=050FEA9F-B064- 4092-B1135C3A70DE1FDA).

9. The Harris Poll #11, *The Religious and Other Beliefs of Americans 2003*, February 26, 2003 (find it online at www .harrisinteractive.com/harris_poll/index.asp?PID=359). Nathan Black, *Poll: 9 out of 10 Americans Believe in God*, April 2, 2007 (find it online at www.christianpost.com/article/20070402/ 26658_Poll%3A_9_of_10_Americans_Believe_in_God%3B_ Nearly_Half_Rejects_Evolution.htm).

.... *About the Author*

Tom Smith lives in Shiloh, Illinois, with his wife, Fran. Both are retired from positions in education and currently they—along with their son, Kevin—serve as directors of the Karla Smith Foundation (KSF). Tom spends much of his time on activities related to KSF, which has a mission to "provide hope for a balanced life to family and friends of anyone with a mental illness or who lost a loved one to suicide."

Tom is the author of five previous books, including *The Tattered Tapestry,* a portrayal of how the Smith family responded to the bipolar disorder and suicide of Karla (Tom and Fran's daughter and Kevin's twin sister).

Tom is an avid, life-long sports fan, with most of his loyalty going to St. Louis teams, especially the 2006 World Series Champion Cardinals. In 1966 he adopted the motto, "Bash on, regardless," which is useful once again in his work for the Karla Smith Foundation.